College Recommendations

Write or Wrong: The Educators' Guide to Successful Recommendation Writing

Edited by Linda Jacobs, M.Ed. and Pauline B. Reiter, Ph.D.

ISBN 0-9676237-1-5

Book design by Tomas Suarez Design
Visit our website at
www.universitypathways.com

University Pathways
5508 35th Avenue N.E., Suite 104
Seattle, Washington 98105

Printed in the USA

ISBN 0-967237-1-5

Preface

Thousands of hours are spent annually writing letters of recommendation for college applicants by already overworked teachers and counselors. As writers of these letters, we want to be supportive; we want to be credible; we want to be honest. We are asked to compare one applicant to another, and we are asked to provide new insights into the individual who has already demonstrated evidence of the rigor of class work, grades, standardized test scores, writing ability, extracurricular and personal activities, and interests.

This book will provide the recommender with guidelines for more effective letter writing. We have surveyed the colleges to learn what value is placed on different kinds of letters, and we have included the results of our survey as well as examples of letters that are useful. Samples of other kinds of recommendations that are poorly written, form letters, sabotage or brave teacher recommendations, damning with faint praise letters, and kitchen sink/overkill letters are also included.

In addition, we offer advice for the student requesting recommendations from teachers, counselors, coaches, employers and others, as well as hints on how to elicit the best possible recommendations.

Finally, we hope the reader will use this book as a resource to assist the student in gaining admittance into the school that is not necessarily the most selective, but the best match for him or her.

Dedication

*To all the caring counselors and teachers who advise,
encourge, and advocate for their students.*

Acknowledgements

Adrian College

American University

Amherst College

Antioch College

Augsburg College

Bard College

Beaver College

Bryn Mawr College

Case Western Reserve University

Catholic University of America

Claremont McKenna College

Clark University

Clemson University

Colorado Christian University

Connecticut College

Depauw University

Emmanuel College

Franklin & Marshall College

George Mason University

Georgia Tech

Goucher College

Interlake High School

Ithaca College

Kenyon College

Lafayette College

Loyola University

Norwich University

Oberlin College

Occidental College

Parsons School of Design

Pepperdine University

Prescott College

Regis College

Rider University

Rocky Mountain College

Rose-Hulman Institute of Technology

San Francisco Art Institute

Seattle Pacific University

St. John's College

Sweet Briar College

The Citadel

The Northwest School

Tulane University

University of New England

University of Puget Sound

University of Southern California

University of Tampa

Westminster College

Special Thanks to:
Jammina Simmons-Wright

Table of Contents

Introduction

There are a plethora of books written for college bound students geared to every phase of the process, from choosing colleges to apply to, to filling out applications and writing essays. There are few such resources, however, for counselors or teachers.

High school counselors are busy people. They assist students with class schedules, deal with discipline and family issues, and help students solve myriad problems. In addition, high school counselors are asked to write recommendations for seniors. Unless students have gotten into some sort of trouble, are superstars, or assertively make a special effort to get to know their advisors, the college counselors may barely recognize the students, particularly at large, public high schools. In some instances, students meet with their college counselors only once or twice and provide them with "brag" sheets or the names of 2-3 teachers who then submit short evaluations for the counselors' use. Once the counselor has amassed this information, how does he or she go about writing an effective recommendation? There are few guidelines to follow.

Teachers, too, are asked to write recommendations for a large number of students. They undertake this time consuming task in addition to their class preparations, teaching assignments, advising of students, and grading of papers. This demand is particularly true for 11th grade teachers who know the students best as they enter 12th grade. Similarly, 12th grade teachers are frequently asked for letters, despite the fact that they have known the students for only a few months. Teachers and counselors endeavor to write recommendations that will be beneficial to their students and helpful to college admission officers. Conscientious teachers take this responsibility seriously, and each letter can take hours to prepare. Again, there are few guidelines.

College admissions representatives are busy visiting schools, holding information sessions, interviewing potential candidates, reading and discussing applications, and participating in making admissions decisions. They note and discount identical letters of recommendation with only the names of the applicants changed. The letter that offers no new insights into the student's ability to succeed at, or contribute to, the institution has limited value. On the other hand, a perceptive description of what makes one student different from others helps institutions to make difficult decisions among many qualified applicants.

How can teachers and counselors best serve their advisees? What kinds of letters are most useful to college admissions officers? In what instances have letters of recommendation been valuable, a waste of both the readers' and writers' time, or downright damaging? When should coach, special talent, employer, or clergy letters be provided? The samples of letters written for applicants that are contained in this book were submitted to us primarily from college admissions officers. They represent letters that had both positive and negative influences on admission decisions. The purpose of this book is to make the writer's job easier by providing guidelines and examples for useful recommendations for students.

Note: Letters have been sanitized by omitting or changing the names of students, schools, and other identifying data. Otherwise, they are presented as they were submitted to colleges.

Useful Letters

Letters that had a positive effect.

- There is no set formula.
- They can be long or short.
- They offer insights not otherwise apparent in an application.
- The writer comes across as knowing the student.
- They show by example - they don't just describe a candidate's qualities.

We have included the greatest number of examples of these letters both because we want to show how helpful they can be and because the purpose of the book is to assist in the production of more effective letters.

Re: Ed

Dear Admissions Officer:

Out of what could be a very lonely background characterized by the frequent absence of his movie-industry-photographer dad and his businesswoman mother, Ed has carved a life of his own, one deeply rooted in his own commitment to hard work. At face value one can easily appreciate his consistent employment, part-time during school and full time during the summer. Though he obviously does not have to work, Ed has held down jobs as a full-time stock boy for Atlas Fabrics, salesperson at Photomore, but most impressively as a first tier salesperson for HiTone Records. These have all been very constructive ways for Ed to spend his time when his school options have all been played out. That's an aspect of his life about which Ed is very proud.

Ed's academic achievements at Blue Cloud School should also be sources of pride for him. Just as Ed has embraced hard work in employment and in the management of his personal life, he has embraced hard work in academics. As the development of his grades and courses over the years indicates, academic success in a school like ours has not come easily. Ed's test scores, in fact, might well suggest that he has performed as a laudable overachiever. In every course he took as a junior, Ed received recognition as a "very hardworking student." For some he's "one of the most hardworking students whom I teach." His "admirable work habits" and perseverance have made each "B" that appears on his transcript a trophy to a maximum level of intellectual and personal output. One teacher in particular chronicles Ed's progress in a way I find most engaging and revealing. His logic teacher speaks for many others when he writes:

> Ed started the course lacking confidence in his ability to analyze and evaluate an argument. He ended the course possessing that confidence. His test scores at the end of the term indicated his achievement. His last unit exam on fallacies was strong, as was his work on the final exam. Ed still finds it difficult to handle arguments in long articles - don't we all!- but he now knows how to attack them with a sense of order and method. His growth in competence and confidence was a pleasure to watch.

That kind of process and success seems to characterize his development in all of the verbal areas of the curriculum.

Fortunately for Ed and for us, the sciences provided him with new windows of opportunity and success. In his electronics class Ed revealed himself to be "very creative" and earned recognition as " a very good student." It was geology, however, that seemed to "light a fire under Ed" and provide him some "glorious" results. His teacher in that subject remarks, "I had no idea that Ed was capable of such extraordinary work. Through hard work and sheer love of the subject, Ed has transformed himself into a top student. I was particularly impressed by his ability to make observations and inferences about rocks and landforms. The entire class recognized Ed as the top geology student. I have taught students with more native ability than Ed, but I have never seen a student with average abilities make so much progress." His progress in both of those courses has heartened and motivated him to take two sciences as a senior, chemistry and physics, and to enrich his love and study of geology through his enrollment in Environmental Ethics. He also has challenged himself by electing to take Pre-calculus instead of Discrete Mathematics. He will crown these curricular advances and achievements with an Independent Study in mineralogy and petrology. Ed has made all of us very proud.

We have gained much from Ed as a contributing member of our community. He has been a generous volunteer to the Downtown Project, a student organization committed to providing educationally social experiences with the children of the area's skid row. Ed also celebrates his membership in OPDADF, an organization dedicated to the promotion of alcohol and drug free adolescent parties. Ed describes this as "my most important extracurricular activity because it allows me to have fun organizing parties, while at the same time, organizing events that are good for the community." In whatever extra time he has, Ed manages to participate on the varsity soccer team and in our rigorous outdoorsmanship program.

Ed has the power of his idealism to propel him forward. He's a wonderfully open and receptive student. He's been a pleasure to teach, and a real tribute to the power of good schooling and good education.

Sincerely,

Academic Dean

Yellow Bird High School
Orange County

Dear Sir/Madam,

I am writing in support of George's application to attend the Topp University. I served as George's high school principal during his freshman, sophomore and junior years at Yellow Bird High School in Orange County. At the end of George's junior year I retired after thirty years in the principalship.

George is a young man with a multitude of talents. In addition to his brightness and high energy level, I believe his major strength is his rational mind which allows him to function in a self-sufficient, independent manner. During my thirty years in the principalship, I've known few students who understand themselves as well as George does. He works off of a strong, positive, basic set of values which includes being painfully honest at all times. He is logical and sensible and at the same time is beautifully creative.

George's responsibility level is greater than most students his age. For instance, as a student George saw the purpose for all academic activities as learning. He was never interested in jumping through hoops to make grades. His grades are strictly a result of his learning, not playing the game to make grades. He lives by his own high standards without ever making a fuss or trying to tell others how they should live their lives.

George is a good athlete and leader. He competes with vigor on the soccer, racquetball and golf teams. On team sports George is an unselfish, steady performer. He plays hard and helps those around him to play their best. George is a quiet, "E.F. Hutton" type leader on and off the athletic field. When he speaks, others tend to listen. It is no wonder that when the Yellow Bird High School faculty was asked to select a few students to meet and dialogue with the Board of Education, George was selected immediately for this challenging activity.

One day when George was a junior, I met with the entire high school student body in groups of about 150 students each to discuss two questions: "What is a civilized high school?" and "How are we doing at Yellow Bird High School?" Since I had assessed George as an exceptionally quiet student, I was surprised that he spoke out several times during the discussions. At the end of the day when we reviewed the day's most significant recommendations and suggestions, it was obvious to me that George was one of the most perceptive, creative and sensitive students in the school. The depth of his understanding of both the problems and the solutions showed that he was a cut above almost all of the other students.

George is a total person. Few people know as well as George what makes others feel the way they do. Even fewer people care as much as George about the way others do feel. He is strong when strength is called for and gentle when being gentle is the solution. He is a bright, hard-working, well-organized academic student. He is a knowledgeable, talented musician. George loves life and lives it in a way that will cause the world to be better place for everybody.

I recommend George to you without reservation. He will succeed academically and he will cause whatever college or university he attends to be a better place.

Sincerely yours,
Past Principal, Yellow Bird High School

Recommendation for Ben

I wholeheartedly recommend Ben for admission. His innate intelligence, balanced academic ability, unusual manner, disciplined work habits, high integrity, and congenial personality make him attractive to both faculty and students alike. I cannot imagine a school environment where he could not excel and thrive.

Ben is a person who might be underestimated at first because he is reserved; however, he can accomplish whatever he sets out to do. He sets high standards and exerts whatever effort is necessary to achieve them. He cannot be predicted with absolute accuracy because he is not quite the passive, conventional person his impeccable manners and steady work habits might suggest. He has a lively mind and an understanding of people which allow him to adapt rapidly to changing requirements or situations. His impressive list of credentials attest to his versitility and talent.

Exuding a quiet competence in his approach to academics, Ben selects demanding courses and meets their requirements without complaint. Though he thinks of himself as a science/math person, he also does very well in Advanced Placement English, a course in which he obviously belongs. Though not particulary loquacious, he expresses himself well in both speaking and writing; I expected the thoroughness in his writing because of his meticulous approach to his studies, but the creativity and humor surprised me. His maturity allows him to laugh at himself and participate in whatever activities may be asked of him. Ben's list of course-related creative activities range from performing as Macbeth in a video parody of "Macbeth" to singing an original ballad before the class. He faces challenges good-naturedly, tries his hardest even at things he doesn't find easy, and accepts crticism and profits from it. He's more grown up than many adults, and this characteristic distinguishes him from many of his fellow classmates.

I think Ben would be a valuable addition to your freshman class next September. If I were to compose an ideal class from the gifted students I have taught over the last seventeen years, I'd want Ben to be one of its members. You will be equally pleased with him.

College Counselor

Recommendation for Mary

There is a radiance to Mary, a human glow, that lights the faces and the spirits of those around her. She is both liked and respected for her goodness. (Yes, her goodness!) I do not even think a wisp of ill will has ever crossed her heart. An understated leadership emanates from this goodness; others, drawn to her warmth, find themselves naturally, happily following her lead. Teachers and students respect her because they know hers is not the indiscriminate, ga-ga goodness of a Pollyanna. Mary is aware of the complexities of this world; she arrived at her bonhomie through philosophical sweat and inquiry. Her acceptance of others means something.

Indeed, for all her sweetness, Mary has real intellectual drive. Her thinking resonates. "Mary brings an almost elegant approach to all her work," says her AP Government teacher. "The insight and precision evident in all her writing are very special strengths. I appreciate her gentle sense of irony and will always remember her barely controlled laughter when we watched 'Lost in America'." The AP Economics teacher appreciated Mary's eloquence, "Mary is a very talented and sensitive student. She writes clear and expressive prose-a rarity in Economics." To the French 4 Honors teacher, Mary was "tranquil and self-reliant, a compassionate, hard worker whose great capacity to concentrate on the task at hand made her a natural leader in the classroom. She kept us on track." The ceramics teacher marveled at the completeness of Mary's artistic persona: "Mary is just amazing. Once she works out her ideas, she starts to work and doesn't stop. She has a great deal of patience, is a mature and responsible student, and is willing to take chances with her ideas. She is also her own best critic and is willing to work and rework something to make it just right. She is so honest with herself that my input is almost incidental." With her probing intelligence and her ability to articulate what she discovers, Mary has all the makings of a future scholar.

Camaraderie and working with people in intensive ways dictate Mary's extracurricular life. Although not a gifted athlete, she has competed for the varsity swimming and water polo teams since tenth grade. She delights in being on a team and will often just hang out with teammates long after practice is over. Last year, Mary organized all the fund-raising efforts for the French Club, monies that were later used for field trips and other social activities. Two summers ago, Mary worked as a counselor at our day camp and as a volunteer at St. Dove's, a program for inner city children. Supervisors praised her gentle, calming touch with the children. The only reclusive activity Mary enjoys is ceramics; last summer she spent the bulk of her time building her portfolio at the Ceramics League.

I recommend Mary with enthusiasm. She is one of our leading lights, giving off a soft, abiding glow.

Director of College Counseling

Recommendation for Steve

When talking with Steve, I know that I am in the presence of a gentle soul. Soft-spoken, self-effacing, quick to see the other person's point of view, he seems if anything, almost too deferential. Watching Steve play linebacker, then, is a revelation. He plays with intensity and intelligence. He does not get overheated, he does not swagger or indulge in macho histrionics, but somehow he invariably makes the first contact with the ball carrier. A Mike Singletary type, he never loses his focus. Small wonder that he was voted team co-captain and first team City League. Typically, when I congratulated Steve on his honors, he smiled sheepishly and gave an "aw gee" shrug of the shoulders. He is a remarkably centered young man.

It could probably be argued that Steve's academic work could use a little more fire. Over the years he has fashioned a respectable, at times commendable, record, but he has never pushed himself to his limits. Part of the reticence may be due to Steve's generally easy going manner. He is interested in the material but he is not inclined to get too worked up about the grades. Another part may derive from a lack of intense intellectual expectations at home. Steve's family wants him to do well and to do the best that he can, but academic excellence is not paramount; that Steve grows to be balanced, kind, and an honorable human being is given equal if not greater importance.

Still, it should be noted that, reticence or no, Steve's record has improved steadily over the past two years. Particularly, his GPA grew from a C+/B- in tenth grade to a solid B in eleventh. This fall Steve raised it yet another notch, moving to a B/B+ in the first quarter. Steve's not sure what academic discipline he will pursue in college, but, with his recent successes in science and with his genuine interest in community, he is giving some serious thought to environmental science.

As might be expected, sports form the core of Steve's extracurricular life. In addition to his success in football, he has also been one of our star halfbacks in soccer since tenth grade. In fact, soccer may be Steve's favorite sport. A captain there, too, he spends his off-season playing for a club soccer team that competes in Junior Olympic tournaments. As he does in football, Steve controls the field; he plays "heads-up ball" and always seems to be in the flow of the game. Teammates count on him to bring the ball up field and spark the offense. As big as sports are in Steve's life, they do not dominate it. An avid member of his church youth group, Steve has traveled to Mexico to build shelters in impoverished communities. Economic necessities have dictated that Steve must earn money each year. As a result, he has held down full-time jobs in each of the past two summers. His mother, a registered nurse, depends on his income.

There is much to admire in Steve. He is a young man of heart, integrity, and talent. I think he has proven he has the intellect to handle a challenging curriculum. There is no doubt that he has the strength of character and the social skills to thrive in a college community. He is a leader by example; he is respectful of all people.

Director of College Counseling

NOTE:
Early decision: Author gears
recommendation to this very
unique college.

To the College Admissions Committee:

I still remember the Sunday afternoon I sat with a cup of something hot and read the *New York Times Magazine* piece about   (imagine—Euclid and Geometry!!); I remember the sense of place better than what was in the cup. I've only known one other person who had a similar sensation, a notion, about learning and how "it ought to be". That person is Robert.

In fact, though Robert wants to file only one application (the horror of placement advisors, of course!), it is the same sort of anomaly I remember from my own college search. I only filed one too, so who am I to give Robert advice?

I guess Great Books draw, inspire, frustrate, satisfy, and intrigue Great Applicants. I have not known many men who appreciated *To the Lighthouse* the way Robert seems to; in fact, I cannot remember another student who talked with me so clearly about it. It must have been interesting to have been Robert all those many years when kids watched TV, chewed gum, and had all those normal, developmental issues. Robert, I think, has most likely always been different, though I have known him — in a remote and peripheral way — for only two years. So, these perceptions of him are like candid pictures a passing photographer might pause over; if it captures some of the differences about him, or essence, it might be useful.

There are two experiences which, though about other characters, describe my impressions of Robert. One is centered around the character in *Never Cry Wolf* who goes to the Arctic to study the wolves, and the other is about the father-son relationship in the odyssey which is *Zen and the Art of Motorcycle Maintenance.* Congruence with these sources is found in Robert's connection with worlds, both internal and external, and with his extraordinary relationship with Joe, his father-dad. When I asked Robert if his own father had to go on a long journey and leave him with a "mentor" (like Odysseus chose with Telemachus), who would Robert hope his father would have chosen, Robert seemed truly thoughtful. And then he could not come up with a single name.

Though I don't mean to over interpret this question in an interview, I do mean to suggest that Robert's relationship with his dad (obvious to a spectator even when the two of them disputed a problem with a clutch repair in Joe's truck) is unique and profound. It almost belittles it to mention it or try to describe it in writing. Suffice it to say that the relationship is deep, genuine, mutually enhancing.

This sort of grounding in one's family (no less important, by the way, is an effective mom and sister) contributes or enhances the kind of presence Robert would bring to the life at Earl College. Though very much his own person, he has a seeker-after-knowledge quality, and though it may have characterized him from the first breath, it's been nurtured and honored in this household always.

The paper mentioned in Dr. Albert's commentary is enclosed with Robert's own documents. Dr. Albert represents perhaps the best "direct" teacher in Robert's school days (which aren't much to write home about as Robert will tell you in his explanation about school to date), and his comment that Robert's spirit of inquiry represents the difference between "a real scholar and a mere pupil".

Though essence is often defiant of capture, Dr. Albert's colleague, Dr. Bruce's comments bring more light to qualities which seem elusive:

Everyone here knows who Robert is. His individualism is evident at first glance (in his dress) and later in his self introductions: Robert literally leaps into people's space and questions them about everything from their evaluation of the latest film release to the U.S. involvement in Haiti.

That's how I met Robert (last year). This year, he is in my English elective, *Contemporary Issues in Critical and Creative Writing*. The first September weekend I brought home a stack of papers from this class, I sat at the dining room table telling my partner, "Robert is an amazing writer." Robert is smart: he makes connections that often no one else in the class is able to make (e.g. the reason a 1930's German Nazi newspaper article was anti-Mickey Mouse).

Robert is intellectually and artistically curious. He is working on a reading and writing project that examines the connections between art and science. He enjoys considering these broad, philosophical issues and finding evidence of them in his everyday life. His poetry is poignant and sharp, using pictures only to tell his stories. (Mr. Karl, senior English electives instructor).

Scholars often have their own sense of time and place and so it is true of this one. When the public school teaches "to the middle" Robert will amble into the library and learn something related, but not in the middle. There is purposefulness in his wanderings since his discoveries, sometimes serendipitous, are his. It is better, he will tell you, than the inane fact-and-memory education which sometimes passes for learning in some schools (perhaps even in ours).

Robert has the critical memory for experience, for feeling and describing the sense of it, for word choice, for cadence. He welcomes the next stage(s), doesn't mind conventional things when they are intentional and useful, but objects to them strongly when they are limiting. If things get boring, Robert refuses to bore himself, and he goes poking about on adventures. Of course, he has often been alone. Nevertheless, his best-remembered (but not quite revered) class before this year was a course in discrete mathematics, which he reports he valued because he "liked Josh and Adam" (the other 2 students in this unusual class of 3). Not a collector of relationships, Robert is nevertheless an appreciator of Genuine Articles, and there is nothing counterfeit about him.

If you don't know these things about Robert, you might (mis)read him as arrogant or withholding. On the contrary, it's more a frustrated hankering after integrity that drives him. Reading the Great Works will continue to provide Robert with the possibility of imitation—a sure way for all writers and thinkers to learn and grow— but even the great masters won't "interfere" (for want of a better word) with Robert finding his own voice and continuing to use it. If we couldn't kill his spirit in public school, he is an Intellectual Survivor! Your school seems a remarkably perfect place for a recovery from schools laden with hall passes, bells and "retrieval, regurgitation, or duplication". (quoted loosely from Robert's essay 1B).

Lest this be too serious, be aware that Robert's humor is the wry sort you see in gifted kids all the time: it's the sudden turn of phrase, the unlikely witticism, the comment out of context but at the center. So, he is a lot of fun to have around, not to pass the time, but to make of time something enduring. Potentialities are only problematic when the climate or environment frustrates rather than encourages them. Those of us who administer educational notions (like descriptions of candidates, recommendations about placements) ought to remember how important routes get to be at Robert's age. He ought to take the road right to your door: I hope you let him in.

All good regards.

Recommendation for Luke

Luke has my wholehearted recommendation for admission. He is a person of unusual intellectual ability and accomplishment; I believe that he can meet the school's demanding expectations, benefit from its programs, and thrive outside the classroom.

Luke was remarkable in the AP English class I taught for his relaxed demeanor; he seemed to exert little effort, but always completed assignments on time and well. He has a distinctive style about him, unlike any other student I have taught. His high energy level and quick mind enable him to make rapid adjustments to changing situations and take advantage of the new conditions before others realize what has occurred. I don't know how to catagorize this talent, but it's very noticeable in class. Luke's ability to adapt and willingness to participate in a wide variety of activities make him a desirable member of the group. Besides, he has an outgoing, warm personality which earns him numerous friends among the faculty and students alike. In some ways, he is still young so I do not think he has reached the academic level of which he is capable. Although he does well now, I believe that he will continue to grow academically in college and beyond.

My assessment of Luke as a student in English is that he is effective in communicating in both writing and speaking. Additionally, he is a talented violinist with considerable training and professional experience, so he is well able to express his ideas through that medium. Neither teacher nor student personalities and styles faze Luke. He works well at his own pace and meets his own standards regardless of the environment. Because of this, he works well in both independent and group tasks.

Luke's unique combination of talent and character seem to enable him to function well in a competitive environment without succumbing to its stresses. A glance at his list of accomplishments will confirm the range of interests he possesses and the level of success already achieved in diverse activities. Luke expects to relate to the world in a multitude of ways, is comfortable with his many gifts, and is frankly, unimpressed with their specialness. An easy person with whom to work, he is generous in the contribution of time and talent to meaningful projects in school. Luke leads sometimes and offers to lead at others, but he never becomes disgruntled if someone else assumes the role of leader. For this reason, as well as many others, he is extremely popular with students and faculty and is sought after as a participant in as many activities as he can fit into his schedule.

I have been impressed with his character as well as his academic and extracurricular interests. Luke is a person of strong conviction and loyalty. He assists classmates whenever possible, and is always honest but kind when dealing with his peers. They seek him out because they know that he will not judge them but will act as a sounding board and be their friend. Luke advocates reason and a restrained consideration of the facts of a matter before emotional response.

In seventeen years of teaching gifted students, I am cautious about whom I recommend for highly competitive institutions. Luke has the academic and personal qualities to succeed. Moreover, he comes from an equally talented family who support his efforts fully and have high expectations for him; they are aware of his ability and encourage him in every way possible.

I think you would be satisfied with Luke.

AP English Teacher

Dear Admission Team:

I love writing about my   Kid, my Cool Scando (should have been Scanda, I guess!), a kid who has proven herself to be one of the leaders, most loved, happiest and most well-adjusted young people at this little school which occupies a little hill in a little state - quite diametrically and stridently different from the long, cold, flat and wide plains of her home. In fact, so "well-adjusted" is my lovely Scando, that Elizabeth almost "sticks out" by virtue of being the All American whole milk, can-you-spell-cow and suck-on-a straw with the blond hair and the blue eyes and the clean cut, upstanding, temperamentally level, smiling, teethy and how-do-you-do greeting each morning. I guess as an Easterner, and originally an inner city foreigner's child, speaking many languages, I still find Elizabeth to be wonderfully "foreign" and almost another species creature, so clean-cut and stand up tall and don't bitch and get the work done kind of a kid. Too long, perhaps have I been used to the super-sophisticate, the borderline, (and de jour) neurotic nerd, the computer dweeb, the socialite's anguish over not having been invited to the "Coming Out" or the chronically brilliant but reclusively independent "brain" or the monolithically myopic "jock" all such familiar "scenes" at a college preparatory school such as this one-or any one.

Elizabeth lights up; she glows. She's so damn healthy and normal I look for signs of stress, or an unhappy face or even, a problem. Nope. And this is not an inane composure of one who is "unconscious"; this is the good old American tough-it-out and stick-to-it attitude of the strong, unspoiled mid-western approach to life. I have found that our "eastern" kids find Elizabeth to have the strengths they really admire, electing her to the captaincy of a highly successful varsity soccer squad (she was four year starter and her passion in sports is soccer, playing off-season for a club team back in her home state coached by a Nigerian international). This former track star (we dropped it) has a good chance of being elected lacrosse captain (she's a three-year starter) and loves doing "the ice thing" for the past two years on our varsity team, a sport which I always remind her must be topologically inbred—after all, ice is the natural formation of choice where she is from.

And speaking of her state, I just love listening to her talk about slicing cheese in a dairy-food store back home, carving chunks off the huge round tons of loafed cheeses, probably garnered from the milk of the cows she deals with when she is working at the other job she's had for the past two summers - working at the State Fair. I mean, do you blame me? What an opening: a cheese slicer in a market which gets its milk locally! I couldn't resist. Could you? The kid is a walking advertisement for a Norman Rockwell bucolic scene of idyllic Holstein wonders; Elizabeth as the Scandinavian Dairy Queen, feedin' 'em, milkin' 'em and cheesin' 'em! Often, I ask her if she would wear a pink and white bonnet and an apron with "Milk: It's good for you" to class one day. She sputters and says something like, "Gosh!".

More than an athletic leader in our community, Elizabeth has given of herself in ways which reflect a reaching out and a caring of others, from her work in our community service programs, to a two-time trip to New Haven in Habitat for Humanity, to working intensely on our AIDS Quilt Committee, to slopping waste in the kitchen, setting up for proms, to being one of the perfects in the dormitories—an especially critical leadership position in our school. But it does not end there—though at times I speak to her about "running too thin" in this community. She is a Big Sister in our in-house peer-guidance program, a yearbook editor and a member of our dormitory committee which establishes policies and procedures for residential living. I find it especially noteworthy that she has chosen to focus her energies in ways which make a significant difference in the lives of others. I don't think there is a selfish, me-first bone in this kid's body. She is tireless, selfless, utterly responsible and almost embarrassingly solicitous of another's needs, wants, hurts.

What is the female equivalent of the Jack Armstrong imago? Is it merely Jane Armstrong? This All-American, mid-western, bright eyed and talented, empathetic and selfless young woman really defines, for me, the strong, forceful and honest qualities of the kind of young person a school is very proud to have taught, coached, advised. You need a bunch of these on your campus; here's a vital one to help you with your "critical mass".

Director, College Counseling

College Evaluation of Jon

Bill and Joan came to Willow Tree School in mid August. As new faculty, they brought with them all the emotions that are associated with starting anew. In addition, they brought with them a new family member: six week old Jon. As a neighbor I had the opportunity to watch Jon grow over the next fourteen years. As is typical of most faculty children at a private boarding school, Jon's growth was strongly molded by the school's environment. The school was his playground. He closely associated with other faculty children (mine included), tagged along with his parents to school events, and was a 'younger brother' to many of the students. Seeing the transition from baby to young adult, I was very pleased to see Jon enter Willow Tree School in the fall.

Now serving as his faculty advisor, I see Jon in a much different light. He is no longer just a member of the 'fac brat pack'. He is a mature young man, ready to make the next transition in life. Both my wife and I have developed a strong fondness for Jon. We look forward to his graduation with mixed emotions: pride in his accomplishments and sorrow at his leaving.

Jon has grown profoundly since his freshman days. What strikes me first and foremost is his willingness to meet challenges and deal with adversity. Since early childhood, Jon had been plagued with a speech impediment. He speaks with a moderate lisp, one which produced great anxiety for him and would cause him to struggle and stutter. In dealing with new people and settings the pain was often unbearable, and Jon found it easier to retreat, much like a caterpillar within a cocoon. I was therefore surprised at the beginning of his junior year to learn that he had auditioned for a small part in a school play. Jon had decided to confront his difficulty head on, and , in winning the part, he forced himself to interact with people. Two more small parts during the school year helped Jon land a major role this past fall in the play, 'You Can't Take It With You'. His was a great performance. Though he struggles with his diction, it is easy to see that Jon's confidence has been bolstered. This past summer Jon had even taken a job for a small company which conducted telephone surveys, again facing directly this need to speak confidently and effectively. His willingness to take a chance has led to his emergence as a leader within the school community.

Academically, Jon is a good student. Because he is a 'fac brat' Jon was raised in a home where his education was readily supported. Jon works hard and has had some great successes. He has also had some great challenges. This past fall, his chemistry was off to a shaky start. He started with a D- at the mid-term in October, but through perseverance and hard work, Jon turned the semester around, earning a C and the December grading period by scoring a B+ on the semester exam. Throughout his four year career at Willow Tree School, Jon has maintained a B/B- average and has scored an 1180 on his boards. I am confident that he is ready for the academic rigors of college.

Jon is realistic about his abilities. Though he plans to major in Business, I know that his 'not too secret' ambition would be to play professional sports: any sport. His love for sports is a passion that is unfortunately not matched by his ability, and Jon would be the first to admit this. I can still see in my mind the five year old boy next door throw ball after ball against a plywood strike zone. Knowing of his passion, it would not surprise me in ten years to see Jon become either a coach/manager of a professional team or a sports writer/announcer.

It saddens me when I realize that Jon is now in his final semester. I have enjoyed working with him, and will miss his being at Willow Tree School, yet I know that he is ready to leave. Jon is academically, socially, and morally prepared for college, and I am certain he can handle the challenges that will face him. I strongly support and endorse Jon as a candidate for college admissions with the firm belief that the fine work he has done at Willow Tree School will continue in his future endeavors.

College Counselor

At a recent meeting of the faculty, the Head of the Upper School described _ _ / as, "perhaps the most mature person at the school -- and I'm including all of you." When it comes to self-awareness (or awareness in general), _ stands alone. Aside from being an extraordinary student (he is very close to the top of the class), _ possesses what some would describe as "a heart and soul quality." His motivations are remarkably pure and his kindness unparalleled. Lest we begin on a too ethereal plane, let me give you some facts. At age fourteen, _ was one of the top junior archers in the nation. He placed third in the Indoor Nationals and qualified for the National Team Trials. Between the ages of twelve and fourteen, _ . lived and breathed archery. He spent every free hour shooting, honing his skill and feeding his passion for winning. Shortly after his freshman year, however, he began to question his goals. His questions led him to the realization that he didn't really enjoy archery, so why did he long to win at something he didn't like? He didn't have an answer, so he put away his bow. During the fall of his sophomore year, he took an introductory ceramics class and it was love at first throw. He discovered a new and better passion, one that he can describe in ways that can make you cry (really, I've seen it happen). As he says, "now I get happy doing what I want, not doing it better than other people. There's always going to be someone who does what I like better than me, so I better make sure I like it."

Now, the faculty at _ . _ might claim that there actually are some things _ does better than everyone else. In AP Spanish, for instance, _ 's teacher described him as "one of the most incredible students that I have ever had in twenty-five years of teaching. His academic abilities are limitless. There are those students who are 'smart' and those who get good grades because they spend ridiculous amounts of time studying -- _ is 'truly intelligent.' However, he not only possesses the gift of intelligence, but he is an extraordinarily wonderful human being."

In English, " _ was writing on a level above most others. . . . I found myself gliding on streams of words, wonderful words, rich and varied and uncommon. . . . I knew I was dealing with a talented English student, one with an ear for language and a mind for examining it for meaning. _ brought a relentless curiosity to class; he always had another question about a scene or a passage under scrutiny." Again, you can't talk about _ 's academic gifts without mentioning his personal ones: " _ has the ability to laugh at the hypocrisies and foibles of others in the most gentle-hearted way. He is exceptionally warm and kind" (English). _ is currently talking about pursuing his love of literature in college, possibly with the goal of teaching -- what a gift to education.

_ has also made his mark in the sciences. In fact, he is one of only a handful of students who have taken the study of mathematics to the level of Linear Algebra -- beyond AP Calculus BC. He was also recommended for the AP Physics classes but couldn't take both of them and continue with all of his art, so he opted for Human Anatomy and Physiology instead. Last year, in AP Biology, his teacher observed that ' _ has the kind of intellectual ability that makes for an excellent student. He is curious and insightful and would stay after class just to talk science. From reading his proposal for a Senior Independent Study project [on an ancient Chinese form of ceramics], I get the feeling this is a renaissance man in the making." And, as always, followed up with these comments on his personality: " _ has his act together. He is confident in his ability and secure. He feels no need to prove his strengths. He often deferred to others and allowed them to answer questions during discussion."

As confident and secure as _ may be, he is never complacent. He continues to find and pursue new intellectual and personal interests. His Independent Study Project has now interested him in the culture and literature of ancient China, which I know he will explore further in college. Athletically, _ still enjoys the personal rewards of golf, but has discovered a new talent. He started running with the Varsity Cross Country team this fall and is a remarkably gifted runner. He was recently featured in the school newspaper with this quote: " _ 's contributions to the team have been extraordinary. He is a natural runner, a pure runner who is genetically made for the sport." What a discovery. He will also be playing on the Varsity Soccer team this year, not as a star, but simply for the joy of playing.

_ comes from a wonderfully grounded family. His father fights fires and his mother designs silk plants (nonflammable, I'm sure), and both are primarily interested in _ 's happiness. There is no parental pressure here. _ is truly self-motivated and takes real pleasure in learning. You can never hold a student as bright, curious, and multi-talented as _ to a vocational goal formed in high school, but he would sure make a heck of a teacher. We know of no higher compliment.

This is a success story in the making. There may not be anyone in the senior class that I am more proud of than _____. Though it may be early to be singing his praises, so far, the academic turnaround demonstrated by _____ and the intellectual maturity evidenced is remarkable. Having turned his attention from the soccer field to the bookshelf, his mind caught on fire. Full of spirit and personality, _____ is also emerging as an enormous artistic talent, with a photography portfolio that is nothing short of amazing for a seventeen year old.

A year ago, _____ was just another student struggling to maintain consistent grades, motivated more by playing soccer than anything else. His junior year started ominously with a depression. _____ found himself totally unmotivated by school. Nothing excited him, and he didn't do any assigned readings: he was getting a D in English. To make matters worse, he developed a physical illness that lasted for a couple of weeks. Then something happened. Seemingly out of nowhere, _____ started realizing the value of learning for learning sake. Attributing his American Literature teacher with making the literature come alive, _____ began reading everything he could get his hands on, from Emerson to Thoreau to Einstein. To further complicate matters, _____ was also diagnosed with ADD in the spring and was prescribed Ritalin. What a difference this made. With greatly improved ability to concentrate and focus, _____'s grades are continuing their upward swing. In fact, _____'s cumulative grade point average through his junior year was around a 2.7. His first quarter senior grades so far come out at 3.9!

Teachers quickly began to take notice of this newly animated and excited student. His American Literature teacher was witness to the biggest turnaround: "Here was a student who by his own admission read mainly Spiderman comic books when the course began and was reading Adrienne Rich on his own when the course ended. _____ *is the student who will keep a teacher in the classroom another ten years hoping to find another one like him.* _____ is not only superbly intelligent reading complex literature, he is deeply intuitive about it." "_____ is probably one of the brightest students in my class," said his Chemistry teacher. His U.S. History teacher also noted a change in motivation: "_____ is genuinely interested in history. _____ was probably one of my more involved students. He was always raising thought-provoking questions, but wasn't afraid to ask the *simple* question either. There is a real love of knowledge where _____ just wants answers to his questions, and he's not interested in the *grade* value."

Not only have his grades turned around, teachers simply love having _____ in their class. "What a sunny disposition! _____ always came to class with a smile on his face. He is not overwhelmed, but seems to take everything in stride...What I admire about _____ is his willingness to be himself; he doesn't seem to bow down to peer pressure," said his history teacher. In Cinema Studies, "_____ practically jumps up and down in class when he's got a point to make or when he discovers something about a film he's already seen or when he sees a new film he loves. _____ participates so eagerly in classroom discussion that there are times when I think of him as a co-teacher, and a welcome one...He knows his strengths and his weaknesses, but let me tell you this: the former far outweigh the latter. I love this kid!!"

This fall Lucien Clergue, the world renown French photographer, came to campus for a speaking engagement. While on campus, Clergue took the time to critique a few student portfolios. Upon seeing his portfolio, Clergue singled _____ out as someone who could immediately turn professional because he "already had the vision." Clergue did not stop raving about _____'s work for the rest of his day-and-a-half visit. This only confirmed what we had already concluded: _____ *is a major talent.* By the end of his junior year, his Advanced Photography teacher commented, "The amount of work and the quality of the work that _____ has been producing these last few months has been nothing short of astounding...His last two series (and it is significant that at his age he is already working in series) came out of his innate interest in people. The success of both series is indicative of the ease and even grace he brings to his social interaction with people. _____ decided to work on a microcosm of _____. He went down to _____ and simply asked people if he could take their photographs...His second series shows an even more complex sensibility at work. He used a large format 4x5 camera and he photographed as many members of his extended family as he could round up...His crowning image is a quadruple (quadruptic?) self-portrait with _____ sitting Buddha-like. And like Buddha, he is buck naked! What a hoot!" His latest series on a friend with leukemia going through various stages of chemotherapy is especially evocative, sensitive, and mature.

_____ possesses a personality that is universally appealing, making him a popular individual to students *and* faculty. His sense of humor, animated presence, upbeat attitude, and gentlemanly manners are endearing to all. Very much reflecting the small-town values and polite manners of his Oklahoman parents, _____ is truly a people person. There is no pretense about this kid; he is completely real. Very open-minded and independent thinking, _____ is content to be himself, despite the grief he might get for his choice of clothes or his haircuts. _____ is honest with himself and everyone around him, and this endears him to all those who know him.

There is nothing more exciting than witnessing the intellectual blossoming of a young mind, and _____ is truly a special case. Full of passion for learning with a distinct artistic eye, _____ is interested in continuing his photography at the college level, but not at the expense of a formal liberal arts and science education. Maintaining a mature understanding of what a holistic education means, _____ wants to continue the exciting process of learning in the right environment for him. The _____ community will dearly miss this young man when he graduates. He has only begun to reveal the tip of the intellectual iceberg in his latest academic performance, and we have complete confidence that this maturity will continue. Be sure to keep your eye on this tremendous creative talent and terrific human being.

Matthew —
This is a great kid!

Associate Director of College Counseling

Statement in Support of the College Candidacy of Carla

"Put Carla in the alpine tundra with a favorite book, and she would be content," says her mother. "At least for a time," responds Carla. Although she loves the outdoors and reads insatiably, Carla also must write, practice karate, organize environmental awareness programs, and participate in other activities close to her heart.

Reflecting on her years at Water View, Carla defines education as "a series of gates, each of which gives us increased access to the world." She feels that her courses afforded her numerous opportunities to explore her interests, but English remains her favorite discipline. Citations for academic excellence, writing awards, published poems, and editorial posts on the fine arts magazine attest to her accomplishment in this field. Not surprisingly, accolades from her teachers abound: "I am in awe of the wonderful ideas that seem to flow effortlessly from Carla's mind" (English 10). "Carla devised her own ending to a Joyce Carol Oates story with a creepy finale a la Stephen King which sent shivers up my spine. Writing is definitely her forte, and she handles analytical essays as deftly as creative pieces" (English 11). In the writing course, Carla's large vocabulary and interest in word usage contribute mightily to the quality of her production. And now, in AP English, the seasoned department chair calls her "an artist, intellectual, and English student with few peers. " Carla also studies Greek mythology in an individualized program where her teacher praises the level of her motivation, adding "Carla only needs me as a guide."

Carla feels that history courses have turned her thinking in unexpected directions. In Asian Civilization, research on topics as diverse as Taoism and the Economics of Viet Nam earned praise from her teacher, who termed Carla " intellectually aggressive". In AP United States History, her love of reading was a tremendous asset, and she approached the course from an independent perspective: " She was able to grapple effectively with a tough essay question on the Battle of Gettysburg with remarkable maturity;, she developed her ideas with informed evidence and created an argument which was both rigorous and thoughtful. This year, in AP Art History, Carla's grasp of the subject matter is "almost intuitive".

Carla's wide ranging interests have caused her to take very full course loads. In Algebra II, where a schedule conflict caused her to miss one class a week, she sacrificed her A. Nonetheless, her teacher praised Carla as "resourceful, creative and responsible." Carla worries less about her GPA than she does about learning. Her independent study in AP PASCAL was, in her words, "...my most challenging course ever. I believed that it would become more and more abstract....Despite all my effort, I struggled, but I also learned limits."

Carla's passion - writing - has shaped her major extra-curricular involvement. She contributes to the features section of our newspaper, but the creative elements of the Fine Arts magazine capture the major portion of her time. Her ninth and tenth grade years each saw three of her poems published; then she joined the editorial staff as a junior. Now she is Joint Editor-in-Chief and has already assembled an active team. Environmental issues matter to Carla, too. A vegetarian who protests cattle raising practices and effects, she is a leader in the Dinosaur/Rain Forest Club. This group sponsors Earth Day activities, organizes our blood drives, and collects coats for the poor.

Always eclectic, Carla has played several sports, but her consistent favorite is karate: "It increases my focusing and concentration abilities as I consider each move thoroughly before making it." In the winter she skis and has won racing ribbons, and in the summer she hikes. Her love of the outdoors has inspired her to volunteer in Rocky Mountain National Park. There she advises tourists about where to go and what to see, assists rangers with their programs, and runs the cash register. This work, too, is "education" for Carla with its lessons about "rivers, flowers, rocks and constellations".

Looking back and forward, Carla says that Water View has allowed her to "hone skills, investigate ideas, search for limits and balance, and grow in many ways." In the future, she plans to "join the Peace Corps., write a book, and travel the world." Possible future professions range from archaeologist to writer to psychologist. Of one thing she is sure, though: the next step is college. She has our enthusiastic support.

Director of College Counseling

NOTE:
This letter is an example of a recommendation for early decision.

Dear Admission Officer:

Her hand shook slightly as she handed it to me, the indentation of a sweaty thumbprint in one corner. "It's ready...oh, no, maybe, I should have stopped on my way here and had my priest bless it!" It can only be Jane's college application. Last year at this time she was struggling with her thoughts about education and its meaning for her life. Then she found Gold College, and ever since there's been a renewed zest for learning.

This playfulness in Jane is something I've recently discovered. All along she's been a serious student, making choices for rigorous coursework and working diligently in classes. Her choices this year confirm her dedication and affirm her commitment to excellence. Jane is not always the highest achiever (grade-wise) in a class, but she is an active, interactive, positive addition.

Jane's strength in school has always seemed to be in English where she has consistently demonstrated the ability to read and analyze, assimilate and respond. Lately though, it is her interest in math which has spurred her on and is leading her to a highly successful first semester.

Her travels during the past couple of summers have convinced Jane that she needs to be knowledgeable as well as wise in order to make the societal contribution to which she aspires. She has evolved into a person with a reputation for benevolence and compassion. Her community volunteer efforts set her apart from the rest of her students.

I worked with Jane this fall on senior class projects and find that she's a good problem solver as well as an active instigator when it comes to getting things done. Peers seem to respect her approval. She is not afraid to get involved and will work determinedly for worthwhile goals.

Jane has been an active member of our swim team which is no easy feat since we don't have our own pool. Early morning (6am) and late night (9pm) practices are commonplace and require true dedication to keep up the pace.

I am really enjoying the person Jane is becoming. She knows when to work hard, when to play hard, how to treat others and how to treat herself. Her parting comment as she left my office was, "I really hope I get accepted. Otherwise my parents will make me apply to Brand X University!" She would be a great addition to your student body.

College Counselor

To Whom it May Concern:

John is the type of person who becomes part of the backbone of a university. John will probably not be your "star" but as we all know, a team takes more than just a star.

John's work habits are outstanding! He is well prepared. His assignments are always done in a timely fashion. "Reliability" and "Consistency" were cited by every one of John's instructors! Other comments included "self-disciplined; conscientious; eager to learn; time well spent; projects reflect planning".

Personally, John is quiet. His teachers quickly assured me "he is reserved but responds." John "contributes". An exceptionally well mannered young man, John is very humble. He is also honest, unusually mature, and possessed of an excellent wit. Every one of John's teachers mentioned how well he gets along with other people, including irritating people.

Academically, John is a good reflective thinker. He is "a strong B student" in his Advanced Placement English class where he is considered above average at analysis but not as strong in writing skills. John, however, is earning one of the only two or three "A's" among 65 trigonometry students. His art instructor wishes aloud "John had begun art earlier." He finds his performance "innovative, creative, and intelligent," emphasizing that John "has excellent drawing and design skills" and "picks up ideas quickly."

John's contributions outside of the classroom have been impressive. Both his school and his community have benefited. John has been varsity basketball manager and statistician for four years. His coach comments, "I'll miss John as much or more than any of the players; he's fantastic! He does everything you could possibly want and more without your even having to ask for it." The community food bank will miss John too. He's been a volunteer there for ten years! He'll be sorely missed by his church as well. He's been an usher for the last three years and held major offices in the Youth Group during that time.

John may not be your star, but he's more essential to the success of your team!

College Counselor

Dear Admissions Officer:

However depleted of merit appear Tom's grades, the grades in no way bespeak the person. Without doubt Tom is Jesuit's best read and most literate senior. Ask him about Jung and he will amaze you with his knowledge, He even delighted his French teacher by writing a witty essay in French about the real father of psychology being Jung. When his government class read the Federalist Papers and undertook to create a mock constitutional convention to rewrite that document, Tom was noted as the scholar in residence on Madison. My discussions with Tom are delightful. Tom is affable, clever, learned, original with language, and full of knowledge. To prepare for his trip to the Soviet Union from December 27 until January 5, Tom has read much Lenin and Marx materials. He read to the point he became a worry to his mother, who envisioned dramatic headlines of defection.Tom has a large body of knowledge, but he has miserable grades. He really cares nothing about grades. Instead of doing trig functions, diagramming sentences, or organizing notes, he is reading the Wilson Quarterly seeking out Slavic insights. At this high school noted for rigid classroom work and country club conservatism, Tom is the odd man, the "flake" to his peers, the one full of integrity.

I cannot say what Tom will do in college. Here he is our best French speaker, wild jazz drummer, intense baseball player, and bane to the academic assistant principal. If I had the luxury of admitting a diverse, mixed, and intriguing freshman class, I would take a big risk on Tom and then hide from those guardians of purity in admissions profiles.

As a student Tom will be teachable, scholarly, and delightful. I am convinced in my old age I'll be reading some interesting political work written by Tom. Someday he might be held up as an example as to why high schools do not work for non-traditional learners. I hope you will take a risk with Tom. To miss Tom is to side step an individual. Down here in conservative city with all these raging capitalists to be and ubiquitous stereotypes, I delight when Tom walks in the counseling office door. I bet he will be worth the risk.

College Counselor

Good People:

My first introduction to Amy occurred a year ago when I drove several students, including Amy, to an Arts and Lectures address by August Wilson. That, in and of itself, says something about Amy. Not many high school students know this talented playwright's name nor are they likely to attend a lecture given by him. Amy had heard of him, and on the way home, the students and I discussed his interpretation of triangular slave trade. We also discussed his intrepid pursuit of a writing career.

Although Amy professes no interest in writing as a career, I envision her writing. She says that she will be an engineer; I see her as a professional word smith. I envy her use of figurative language, her gift of phrase, her mastery of literary illusion. Whichever career she pursues in and out of university, her writing skill (or talent) will aid her.

Her energy and organizational skills will help her as well. Recently, I overheard one of her classmates refer to her as being "perky as a squirrel." The old-fashioned simile amused me, but it is apt. She dashes from place to place, always doing something productive. If she isn't on her way to cheerleading, she is hanging signs in the hall, planning an activity for the senior class, or arranging photo sessions for the yearbook. She also brings that bustle into the classroom with her. During writing workshop time in my Expository Writing class, she proofreads her classmates' writing, consults with me, strides over to the dictionaries or Thesauri to check words, or occasionally asks to follow a lead in the library. She uses time very, very efficiently.

I will remember Ms. Amy, a leader in this high school's academically strong senior class, as an adroit student, competitive as needed, cooperative as needed, diligent and intelligent always.

English Teacher

RECOMMENDATION FOR DAN

Independent, a true individual, focused yet not bound by conventions, reliable, somewhat aloof—these are the words that come to mind when I think of Dan. With Dan, what you see is what you get. There are no surprises here.

Spring High School is small, sometimes cliquish, and very competitive. Students are concerned—about themselves, about their futures, about the condition of the environment, about those less fortunate and yes—about what college they are going to. This is good and this is bad. They should be concerned about life after—that's the good part. They shouldn't be so concerned that it overtakes their day to day lives. Dan has chosen (he's somewhat in the minority here) to approach the college selection process pretty much like he approaches most things—rationally and clinically. That's o.k. because that's Dan.

Last summer, Dan was fortunate to be chosen for the Youth Science Exchange Program through   University. He and about 30 other students spent three weeks in Australia studying regional zoology and marine biology. It was an excellent opportunity for Dan to "test the waters" in this possible field of study while earning some college credit. Dan is a gifted math and science student and well suited to a career in this area—should he choose it. He has taken honors and AP course all four years and just finished first quarter with a 3.8 GPA in a perfectly balanced senior schedule. Keep in mind that he doesn't get "credit" for advanced courses in our unweighted system. If he did, his rank would be higher.

Dan has been an active member of our sports program here at Spring High School. He has lettered in soccer, racquetball, and golf and while he does well in all these areas—again, he hasn't exactly chosen the high profile sports. He's also a contributing editor for our alternative school newspaper and has played the guitar for four years. Mike, Dan's guitar teacher, has commented on Dan's willingness to learn and on his commitment to our music program. He has been in jazz band and last year earned an A in AP Music Theory. Musically, he's come a long way in a short time.

Dan is not the typical student. I admire him because he has taken advantage of the opportunities here while maintaining his academic and personal freedom. His excellent sense of humor and honesty is appreciated by the faculty and his peers. Dan will be a contributing member of a college community—but without fanfare or having to draw a lot of attention to himself. He's completely comfortable with who he is and where he's going. We wish him well and are pleased to offer our strongest support on his behalf.

College Coordinator

Recommendation for Joe

Joe has been a member of my sophomore English, Junior Classical Studies, and senior English courses. He tells me that his favorite courses have been Classical Studies for its strange mythology and literature, U.S. American History because it provided him with the American story, and Chemistry because it allowed him to discover things on his own and to see how things work in nature. He is well known at the school for his ability on the varsity soccer team.

Joe's non-academic experience is interesting because it offsets his apparent ingenuousness. When he was 12 or 13 years old he worked at a local dog-and-cat care facility where he learned that animals are "not all cute and fuzzy." He also worked as a counselor in the CSU Summer Program (he admits when pressed that he was the athletic director for the small chidren.) In that capacity he learned that the children likewise were "not all cute and fuzzy." I asked him what he did with recalcitrant children and he talked about his strategies and limitations. I was particularly impressed to hear that he knew not to become angry but to refer difficult cases to the director. His latest job, working for the Parks Department, put Joe in touch with manual laborers and the homeless whose lives differ greatly from his own. As a result of his experiences, Joe took a course in CPR. Joe is in fact remarkably aware of his own specificity, unlike many students who cannot imagine that others are much different from themselves. As a sophomore he played soccer for "Teen USA," but he is more likely to talk about the foreign students he met than about the games. (He was quick to list their countries of origin in our interview—Sweden, Holland, Denmark, Bolivia, Spain, Germany, Israel, and Canada.)

Joe's academic performance has been average, but he is free of the common ploys that one frequently finds in others of similar ability—he never carps for a higher grade, blames teachers, or makes an industry of excuses. Joe readily acknowledges his weakness and attends tutorials to improve his English. He has difficulty with spelling; he hesitates to use punctuation that he does not understand; he would rather write plot summary than analysis. Even so, I can say that he has begun this year to interpret action, events, and dialogue in literature and, in fact, he shows valid insight on those occasions. He does not like to risk unknown territory but, on the other hand, he does not bluff.

When asked, "What adjectives describe you best?," Joe answered "humble, caring, warm, giving, considerate." That makes sense to me.

I recommend Joe for his honesty, humanity, and industry.

English Department

To Whom It May Concern:

Lisa represents the best of the best. She is one of the most creative thinkers I have encountered in my ten years of teaching. She is smart, warm, empathetic, passionate, articulate, and disciplined. Her loves are diverse and many; a love for learning, a love for the written word, a love for humanity, and a love for what is right. I am pleased to give her my highest recommendation.

I have known Lisa for the past one and a half years. She was enrolled in my college preparatory Junior English class last year. However, to put her in the same category as most other students would be a mistake. She is one of a handful of students who approachees learning as a true fifty-fifty partnership. For every book we studied as part of the curriculum, she made personal suggestions for ways in which the curriculum or my own reading background could be enriched. At the end of our study of Native American literature, she suggested Dan Milman's ever-popular "The Way of the Peaceful Warrior". After our reading of some contemporary fiction, Kingsolver's "Bean Trees", she suggested "Animal Dreams". And the list goes on.

Lisa pushed me to be a better teacher because of her unquenchable thirst for more—more knowledge, more understanding, more connecting. An in-depth discussion on anything we read would not be complete if Lisa didn't challenge us to look at a character or an interpretation in a different light. Each writing assignment was tackled with such energy on her part! If, for example, the assignment was for a student to look at Jay Gatsby's character and argue the cause and the point of his downfall, Lisa searched for more depth—we must look at the society, its influence on him, and his influence on it, too. We can't separate man from his environment, she'd argue. And she was right, always right.

So she'd work on her new, improved assignment, stopping by my office when she got excited by another idea, another insight on her part, smiling, talking fast, writing even faster, hitting on the multiple layers of complexity that each work we had studied. Then she'd want to convey her analysis in some unique style to Lisa. Again, in her Gatsby paper, she carried throughout an image of a glass house shattering when discussing the delicate world around Gastsby shattering, too. I marveled at how much she was able to do on her own. She really understood that truly good pieces of literature were tapestries of words, images, and ideas woven together. She, too, would be in awe at how skillfully woven these tapestries were. Because she had this keen understanding, she would try her talented hand at creating her own tapestries. What a joy it was for me to witness her discoveries over and over again.

I truly believe that one of the reasons that Lisa is able to appreiciate the depths of people is because she lives such a rich life. Yes, she is a voracious reader, but she does not live vicariously through anyone, fictionally or not. She evaluates her life and her values and consistently seeks to improve both. Because she carefully studies how she lives her life and is so willing to give of herself, whether through discussion, through hard work, or through her volunteer work at a nursing home, we are enriched by her.

I am proud to know Lisa. She is an exceptional young woman.

Sincerely yours,
English Instructor

Recommendation for Alan

Alan, one of my top AP students this year, is a model student in every respect. He exhibits intelligence, clarity and originality of thought, organizational skills, a genuine interest in learning, and the willingness to go the extra mile in doing an assignment well.

Alan has a straight A average this year, an A he could have earned doing even less than he does, not because the class isn't demanding, but because Alan goes far beyond a given assignment. For example, while we were studying the modern McCarthy novel, *All the Pretty Horses*, I briefly discussed existentialism as a philosophy manifested in the work. Alan went out and read Jean Paul Sartre on existentialism and, in his paper on the McCarthy novel, discussed how five of Sartre's points were applicable to the novel. While studying *As I Lay Dying*, Alan, on his ever present laptop computer, was pulling up critiques on the novel as we went along, comparing his own interpretations with those of the critics. He's an original thinker as well. In a paper on *The Odyssey*, Alan compared a book of "The Odyssey" to a movement in a Paganini opera.

Alan is a scholar, a genuinely curious student and a gentleman. Immaculately groomed, serious yet witty, personable and bright, Alan is an asset to the class. I truthfully cannot fault him in any way. He is a bright spot in my day.

AP Literature Instructor

GLISH TEACHER RECOMMENDATION FORM

lease return directly to the   College Admissions Office within two weeks.

Transfer students please note: Only two recommendations, on official letterhead, are required. One should be from an instructor in your proposed academic discipline. See application instructions for transfer students.

? THE APPLICANT
ill in your name and address below. Detach this page and give it to a teacher who knows you well and has taught you in an academic discipline within the last two years.

Name of applicant _____
                        Last   First   Middle

Address _____
              Street   City or Town   State   _ip Code

Applying for   ☒ freshman   ☐ transfer   ☒ fall   ☐ spring 19____   **Application Deadline:** _____

TO THE PERSON COMPLETING THIS FORM
The Admissions Committee would appreciate your candid evaluation of this student as an applicant to   College. Your appraisal of his/her academic attitude and performance, motivation, intellectual ability, study skills, and critical reasoning will be of great help to us in reaching a decision in his/her best interest. Under Public Law 93-380, the Family Educational Rights and Privacy Act, candidates for admission to   College do not have access to their records in the Admissions Office unless and until they enroll at the college. To assure confidentiality of information within the spirit of the law, we will destroy this form and any other subjective supplementary statements about this student before his/her matriculation at

1. In what course(s) have you taught this applicant?   JUNIOR ENGLISH

2. Is this course   ☐ advanced placement?   ☐ honors?   ☒ college prep?   ☐ regularly paced?   ☐ remedial?

3. How much outside work is required for this course? (approximate hours per week)   ☐ 0-1   ☐ 2-3   ☒ 4-5   ☒ More than 5

4. Please describe any long-term projects.   AFRICAN-AMER. + 19thC. WOMEN WRITERS

5. Is the applicant's work prepared promptly?   ☒ Always   ☐ Usually   ☐ Sometimes   ☐ Never

   Does the applicant participate in class?   ☒ Frequently volunteers   ☐ Sometimes   ☐ Only when called on   ☐ Never

7. What is the strongest aspect of the applicant's written work?   SENSITIVITY, INSIGHT, OPEN-MINDEDNESS, KIND-HEARTEDNESS

8. What is the strongest aspect of the applicant's oral work?   LISTENS, ALLOWS OTHERS SPACE TO CONTRIBUTE, GENEROSITY + INSIGHT

9. How would you rate this applicant as compared to other students?
   ☒ Truly outstanding (top 10%)   ☐ Above average   ☐ Average   ☐ Below average

If you would like to receive   departmental information in your field, please check.   ☐

                                                    (AM)

Name (please print or type) _____   Title   ENGLISH

Signature _____   Date   12.2.95

School or college _____SCHOOL_____   SCHOOL

Office telephone (____)_____ _____-_____   Office fax (_____)_____

School address _____HILL ROAD_____
                          Street

_____
      City   Watts   State   Zip Code
                                                    Continued on back

RECOMMENDATION FOR

I imagine that with the reams and reams of paperwork devoted to student evaluation and candidacy that it must sometimes feel like the same descriptive words and choice phrases are being coined and utilized; viz: "Viable candidate" so and so is a "bright and able student" who, without a doubt, "shows tremendous promise" and will, if not in the near future then certainly by graduation time, "grow to become a significant contributor to the college community." As one who has sifted through the memory banks for unique, characteristic anecdotes and choice, personal words, I can say honestly that somewhere after the twentieth recommendation distinguishing traits and achievements can unknowingly stray into the generic, depersonalized realm. With this said, I clearly, unequivocally, with knowing-consciousness choose to invoke the following words:

is one of the most OUTSTANDING, truly **OUT-STANDING** candidates for whom I have written evaluation/recommendation.

This phenomenal young man is one of the most generous, kind-hearted, considerate, compassionate, thoughtful, diligent, humble, insightful and tenacious human beings with whom I have had the pleasure and HONOR of interacting. TRULY. I can go on and on about   : I can mention his remarkable musical/Jazz drumming ability; I can mention his sensitive, thoughtful, POWERFUL unit projects on Frederick Douglass and late nineteenth-early twentieth century women writers; I can mention his generosity of spirit and mind in class and in clubs, his irreplaceable contributions to the   community service initiatives as well as other service organizations; I can mention his maturity, his leadership, his humility and concern for others over self; I can mention, I can mention. This is a REMARKABLE young man who WILL, **GUARANTEED**, shine and succeed in all that he undertakes. The truly fortunate school that offers the most attractive package to   will enroll one of the most balanced, WHOLE students imaginable.

If I can be of further assistance in this matter, please do not hesitate to call me.

Dear Admissions Committee:

The most appropriate phrase to describe Ann is "perfect balance." During the two years I had her in class, I was amazed at her ability to manage the academic, extracurricular, social, work and family aspects of her life.

Using excellent time management skills, along with high motivation and a strong desire to achieve, she was one of the top students in my trigonometry class. She frequently organized small study groups which benefited the students by giving them extra math practice and also by giving them the opportunity to teach each other — the best learning experience there is. Ann's current math teacher informs me she is continuing to organize the small group study sessions after school. I have had the opportunity to observe Ann outside the classroom; that is, at the location of her part-time employment and with the environmental club which she leads. In both these situations, Ann displays the confidence, the enthusiasm, and the poise which make her a truly remarkable woman.

Ann's manners are so impeccable they seem to come from an earlier, more gentle and civilized time. Yet she in no way stands apart from her peers. The perfect balance I spoke of earlier allows her to be a fun loving, sociable teenager without compromising her strong sense of values. She is in control of herself; she knows what direction she wants her life to take. You will love having this beautiful young woman as a part of your student body. She will be an asset and an inspiration.

Respectfully submitted,

Math Department

To Whom it May Concern:

"Solid" is the theme of Jeff's career here at the Academy, where he has worked very hard to become a reliable, conscientious student and contributing citizen. His great gift is his love of learning, and while his external successes may appear modest, the heart that goes into his endeavors is grand and vast.

Jeff's teachers respect him and his steady progress in many disciplines:

> Jeff is a wonderful young man, hard-working, thoughtful, self-aware. He is growing in confidence in literary analysis, writing steadily more effective essays. He picks hard topics, and may sometimes bite off more than he can chew, especially under time constraints, but the complexity of his intentions is admirable. He is consistently prepared for class and participates insightfully in discussion. (English IV AP)

To another senior-year teacher, Jeff's impressive sincerity and engagement are as important as his improvement in the coursework itself:

> Jeff is one of the leaders of our classroom conversations because learning really matters to him. He has respect for others. His honesty thus far has been most impressive. Our aim is to get students thinking for themselves to the best of their ability; Jeff is well on his way to that goal. (Humanities)

Several factors in Jeff's life support him in his self-discipline and work ethic. His religious faith and commitment to service, exemplified most recently by his participation in mission trips to Central America, are important sources of meaning and satisfaction for Jeff, who wears his faith quietly and deeply. Also, Jeff will be the first in his family to pursue and complete a college education. These factors account in part for the way Jeff's strong drive to succeed academically is tempered by a gentle, humane, loving approach to his family and community.

Jeff has had to find his own path, build his own road to the next step; no family tradition—other than goodness and hard work—has paved his way. We admire him most, perhaps, for how thoughtfully and genuinely he has made his choices and lived his life so far, whether in academics, basketball, student government, or community and church service. Jeff says of himself, "I find great joy in devoting myself wholeheartedly to the things in life which I see as important." We find great joy in acknowledging and applauding that devotion and wholeheartedly recommend him.

College Counselor

NOTE:
The last paragraph directs recommendation to a specific university.

Letter of Recommendation:

Over the past four years I have served as Heather's college counselor, academic advisor (junior year) and varsity softball coach. These roles have allowed me a unique perspective in order to assess something of Heather's personality and character.

This is an independent, strong-willed young woman—outspoken, stubborn on occasion, straightforward, socially gregarious, mature, perceptive, devoted to people and tasks that matter to her—one who cuts her own path, regardless of the peer pressure of the day. Clearly, over the past four years, Heather has emerged as a student leader—without fanfare. For example, three of the past four years she has been elected class vice-president; during the past two years, she has captained the cheerleaders; and this spring she will be in the running for co-captain of varsity softball. Heather knows how to set goals and follow through. She is equally comfortable with adults and peers. Not only an avid conversationalist, but a good listener, Heather is a supportive confidante and one who seeks ways to spark spirit and well being in this community.

It may be helpful to indicate here that Heather's childhood and adolescence have not been easy. She has weathered three failed marriages and the trials and tribulations of helping parents and a now five year old brother. On occasion she has had to shuttle between Mom's household here, grandparents in the South and her biological father's home in the West.

Heather has learned much about herself, about the nature of family and the need for resourcefulness and self-reliance. Despite a considerable amount of emotional hardship, she remains fundamentally upbeat, charitable—a warm, caring friend to many. Last year she wrote a powerful opening to an autobiographical essay I ask of all juniors: "When I think of what stands out about myself as an individual, I have come to the conclusion that the ability to forget the past and overcome hardship is my greatest strength...I have not allowed the past to interfere with my present, nor will I let it interfere with the future. I am determined to succeed, independently, and owe nothing to anyone, except to my own perseverance."

Academically, Heather stands in the middle of a senior class of forty. Humanities and social sciences seem to foster the greatest interest and reveal strengths. Given her verbal acuity she is often a discussion leader; comfortable expressing herself, she relishes the give and take of the classroom. On paper she writes sound exposition. Her interest in people, in psychology as a discipline, allow her thoughtful literary insight.

One faculty comment instructively illustrates in part Heather's academic demeanor (and her personality as well). Last year her American history teacher, the department chair, wrote: "A very important member of my second hour class...I don't know that I'll ever be able to admit to my professional colleagues that I allowed her to write a paper on the historical and social importance of disco, but to my surprise, she came up with its relevance and managed to produce a fine paper, one that clearly placed the music in the context of the 70's....It surprised me how she took this seemingly facile topic and brought credibility to it." Heather has begun the year strongly—her best start ever, in fact. Her current performance and attitude are positive indicators of continued success.

I have never seen Heather as excited about anything in her life as I have about her discovery of Fineman University. She recently visited the campus, bringing her father from the West. Atmosphere, academic program and location all appear to fit her needs. Heather will bring the quality of involvement, the initiative and integrity, and the force of personality we have experienced here. Importantly, she will be the first member of her family to receive a college diploma. In this spirit I recommend Heather enthusiastically and without reservation.

Director of College Counseling

RECOMMENDATION

a new student at   High School has become one of the most creative and talented members of the class of   transferred from   High School for his senior year enabling him to participate in the International Baccalaureate program.   came with a strong record in athletics, academics and service group experience. As a ninth grader, he participated in both cross country and track and as a tenth grader continued track both in the winter and spring seasons and was a member of the junior varsity football team. At   High,   was a peer counselor and was a member of S.A.F.E (Stopping Aids for Everyone) as well as a member of the Youth and Philanthropy Club and the Art Club.   In eleventh grade he continued to participate in cross country and varsity winter track. He was named president of S.A.F.E and continued membership in both the Philanthropy and the Art clubs and joined the Pythonian Society. This year   also tutored elementary school students on a daily basis after school.

          is an extremely talented young man who has had two of his poems published. His literary skill has been noted by the staff at   and he is currently enrolled in the senior portion of the International Baccalaureate English class. But English is not the only area of expertise for   His math level and science level are extremely strong. He was able to move into the International Baccalaureate Finite Math class as a senior, along with Functions, IBH English 12, IB Anthropology, IB Art and IBH Theory of Knowledge. Upon coming to   sought out the people who were involved in our school with AIDS awareness and he is now currently working with Ms.   Family Life and Physical Education Coordinator to start our own   at   High School.

Outside of school,   has worked as a waiter and at the   Bakery. He now volunteers at the   Hospital and during the summer of his junior year, he travelled to Spain where he stayed with a Spanish family and was able to make friends and immerse himself in the culture of another country. This last experience is a good example of the kind of young man   is, always open and ready to gain from new experiences. Changing schools as a senior is not an easy task, yet I have observed   and seen him as a student who has quickly moved into the academic and social milieu of this suburban academic and culturally diverse high school. In his soft-spoken way and his easy manner, he has become a favorite both of his classmates and his teachers. He is able to relate to them and has added a wonderful dimension for us at .

          has joined in the civic groups, the club activities and will add a new dimension to our school by heightening the awareness of the tragedy of AIDS among our young people. As his counselor for the past few months, I have come to know   and respect him as a young man with great potential, a wonderful heart and a spirit that is rarely found in young people these days. It is often difficult when a student transfers, to equate the grade point average or the courses taken with the previous school and I can tell you that   has been able to work in to our most rigorous International Baccalaureate classes and achieve at a level commensurate with students who have been in our program for four years.   grades have shown a marked improvement since the 9th grade. His current interims are very strong and this should be his strongest year yet. However, in the transfer, his grades from   which were graded on a 5 point scale will not average out to a comparable grade point average for those of us who are on a 4 point scale. Therefore, I urge you to not look at this young man's GPA but rather concentrate on what he has done and his standardized test scores. I believe, from my more than twenty-five years experience in the field, that   will be a member of the class of the year   that will truly bring your university something unusual, talented and definitive.   has the intellectual capability, the ability to sustain interest, study and commitment to be one of your finest students.

Dear Sir or Madam:

At Mountain Top School about eighty percent of students go on to four year colleges, while only about thirteen percent go to community colleges. Thus, you can imagine how competitive Mountain Top School is. It is therefore refreshing to have a student such as Kate who is delightful, charming and unassuming, yet one who is serious about her academic work and diligently completes every assigned task.

In my English 3 Honors class during the first semester, Kate was not the strongest student. She needed to take more risks and to venture into more probing analysis. At the end of the first semester, she received only a "B". However, for the second research paper, she chose to write on the American novelist Louisa May Alcott and two of her novels. She enjoyed reading those novels and was amazed at the unusual life Alcott had led because of her eccentric father, Bronson Alcott. This paper was an improvement over her first in that she showed she was capable of positing a thesis, providing more than ample development, as well as excellent documentation. She should have little difficulty writing at the college level.

Outside the classroom, Kate has sought to develop her acting talents. She has performed semi-professionally in community theaters. Last semester she was one of only three actors in a play entitled "The Sacrament of Meatballs". She found the play unusual, and she enjoyed the experience even though she found she had to effect a delicate balance between fulfilling her scholastic responsibilities as well as her stage responsibilities. For example, during rehearsals, she spent as many as thirty-four hours in training. She also performed in a one-act play last year and was an assistant director for two months. When I asked Kate to tell me which activity she most enjoyed in high school, I was not surprised when she said she loved acting because she enjoys "performing and being dedicated to the theater." Besides being involved in the theater, she also played tennis during her freshman and sophomore years and was voted "Most Improved Player" both years. She has also played the piano for five years, although not competitively.

Kate's family background is somewhat unusual in that she is Arab-American. She says being bicultural encouraged her to read frequently, to form her own opinions on events, and to become more aware of nature. Also, because of her cosmopolitan background, she spent a month in France last summer visiting the country with a friend who lives there.

Her family is currently struggling with the fact that her grandmother suffers from Alzheimer's disease, and Kate along with the rest of her family, has had to deal with the emotionalism of that devastating situation.

Kate will bring many personal and academic gifts with her to college.

College Counselor & English Teacher

Recommendation for Joel

Looking for structure and less clutter in his life, Joel came to the Macintosh School from Rain Tree as an eleventh grade residential student. He chose Macintosh in order to take advantage of the school's Academic Learning Skills Program. The program allows college-bound students to remain in the academic mainstream while learning to compensate for a disability. Diagnosed with Attention Deficit Disorder, Joel wanted to sharpen his focus by retraining his intellect rather than by using medication. Reflecting on his choice, Joel remarks that he could write volumes about the changes he experienced in the course of his first year at Macintosh "the most difficult and intense restructuring I have ever gone through". Not the least has been his changed attitude about the place of athletics in the life of the mind. As a coxswain in boy's crew, he can now appreciate the value of athletics in focusing both energy and desire in pursuit of a goal.

Joel's teacher in the Academic Learning Center sees him as "a tremendous thinker, someone who loves to philosophize and debate..". In fact, along with a number of other extracurricular activities, he became president of the philosophy club in his first year at Macintosh. His teacher goes on to observe that Joel has shown great improvement in his ability to argue a point effectively and clearly. Socially aware and ethically moral, he is not afraid to speak his mind or to adopt an unpopular stance. In this sense he is an intellectual leader. He is not afraid to pick a difficult (but interesting) topic to research and write about.

His eleventh grade English teacher was similarly impressed and described him in almost identical terms: "Joel is a very bright, independent thinker who loves to read and philosophize about what he has learned." Although these qualities are not always evident in his grades, they are apparent in his interpretive approach to studies. More of an intellectual than a student, Joel has needed reminders about proofreading his papers and watching his signage in math, where a plus or a minus can make all the difference. At the same time, he can be very creative, preferring, for example, to use his own rather than conventional strategies to solve math problems. Usually he arrives at the answers in geometry more quickly than do his peers, although the opposite is true in algebra.

Joel's parents are both professionals. His father is an accountant and his mother, a lawyer. Joel learned something about law himself when he obtained a summer job as a law clerk, the same summer he attended Land's "Ready for College" program. He found the schedule at Land very intense with writing assignments every night, but the regular exercise has conditioned him to write freely and fluently. Considering a variety of possible college majors, from Anthropology to Business, Joel has shown truly outstanding academic creativity, self-confidence, sense of humor, personal initiative and social tolerance. In an effort to realize his considerable intellectual potential, he has chosen the hard way. Through self-discipline and training rather than medication, he is trying to overcome ADD and become more streamlined in thinking and action. We cannot but admire both his character and his intellect and enthusiastically recommend him.

Director of College Counseling

Rich in detail you know the student.

has to be one of the most adaptable, responsive and straight-forward students that I have worked with in many years at our high school. He has been able to elect a demanding battery of teachers and subjects, and this year is no exception. He is off to a real fast start. I would say that his rank in class is not a true reflection of his real ability to handle a strong academic experience. Certainly his junior C.E.E.B.'s--710 verbal, 680 math--indicate that the ability is there. When you add Achievements--English 680, Math 660--you have a young man who has some high potential for academic excellence. He is a fellow who is on the move. I asked him to list a few adjectives which he, his family or friends would use to describe him, and he answered:

"Responsible--I cook my family's meals and do all the shopping. My brother and I clean the house, and whatever else needs to be done. Friendly--I have a lot of friends, and I like to spend time with them. Laid-back--I don't get excited over little things. Independent, self-reliant--I know how to live by myself, my father travels a lot. Adaptable--I have shared a small room with my brother in an apartment, and I've lived in a three story house. My parents' divorce has made me adaptable."

His parents divorced a few years back, yet he and his brother have been able to make the adjustment. He has to be one of the most welcome and mature students that I have worked with in many years at our high school. I asked him to describe any events or circumstances in his life that had contributed to making him the person he is today. His answer came back quickly: "My parents' divorce made me a much more mature person."

Another question: Describe an adult in your life whose values you respect: "My grandfather. I admire him because of his many varied interests (professor of German, farmer, archaeologist)."

is not afraid to go to work, go above and beyond what is asked of him. He has been a very subtle and moving force here at our high school. Typical of his drive and tenacity is the fact that he was the founding member of our Boys LaCrosse team.

Hard working, realistic and a young man who is keeping his options open appear to be the best descriptions of this young man. He certainly has my enthusiastic endorsement as a young man who can handle a challenging post-secondary school experience.

Dear Friends,

Ryan has asked me to write a letter of recommendation in support of his application to Stately College. It is a pleasure to do so knowing he will make splendid contributions to campus life. Ryan is excited about Stately because of your program for special needs students and I cannot imagine a more dedicated or optimistic young person starting out a college career.

Because Ryan's teachers can say more about his academic accomplishments, I wish to highlight his strength of character. Watching Ryan grow over the years assures me that he is prepared to face many kinds of challenges. For a person with learning problems, one may not be surprised if he or she is frustrated or "turned off" to academic studies. Ryan has a desire to succeed that is remarkable. Not deterred by circumstances, he has been able to set goals and meet them. Just the fact that he is preparing to attend college reflects his commitment to education when an easier alternative might be tempting.

Perhaps the best example of Ryan's maturity is his involvement with the Boy Scouts. To achieve the distinction of Eagle Scout Ryan mastered an extensive variety of skills and knowledge: yet more important, he has consistently shown leadership skills unusual for someone his age. Not content to excel only in his own regard, Ryan has worked tirelessly to teach younger scouts and provide guidance on community projects and wilderness adventures. He is patient with others, considerate of their needs, always ready to lend a shoulder or contribute ideas. It seems that Ryan is well on his way to attaining a balance many adults never reach: how to find one's appropriate place in a community of citizens.

In a society where we often doubt the values of young people, Ryan gives us confidence about the future. He will seek new opportunities and make the best of them. I believe Ryan will be a fine asset to Stately College.

Sincerely

HIGH SCHOOL *addresses desire to succeed*

LETTER OF RECOMMENDATION FOR

_____ is a rather quiet person. He is a very good athlete and especially dedicated to the sport of football. He has faced an injury which has cost many other players their career because they did not have the will or desire to rehabilitate. In _____'s sophomore year he "blew out" his knee on his very first varsity play. He had worked very hard to get that opportunity and then it was gone. To give you some idea home tough he is, the injury happened on Friday night and he didn't acknowledge the extent of it until he collapsed on it Monday afternoon.

Coming back from such a serious injury is always difficult. _____'s recovery was complicated by a torn hamstring just as he was starting to make real progress. Through sheer determination he won a position on the starting defense in his senior year. He is probably more proud of this accomplishment than any thing else he has ever done. And while it no doubt took away from time that should have been devoted to improving a rather light grade point average, it is still a true measure of _____'s ability to focus on a selected area.

_____'s testing history indicates that he has much more ability than he has shown in his grades. It should be noted, however, that _____ has started to show academic improvement at a time when his peers are showing signs of relaxing. While he still shows weakness in English, he has elected to take a very challenging Physics course which has been a "killer" for more than a few of his classmates. I think he should be able to perform to the standards you expect at _____ College and I recommend _____ for admission.

COLLEGE RECOMMENDATION

Laura is presently in my Honors Institute for Leadership in Life class. The format of the class involves discussion and analysis of the major issues and developments of our day. Much research, reading and writing are required for the course. In addition, the curriculum and its activities are designed to promote self-confidence and leadership skills. Laura has been a very good student in the class this year.

Laura seeks to learn as much as she can, both in and out of the classroom; she tries to develop a complete and balanced understanding of the subject matter. Laura is blessed with fine abilities in analysis and synthesis. She shows insight and thought on all ideas and topics, demonstrating evidence of independent reading. The research she does for her papers has been very good, as has her written work offering her opinions and backing up her ideas with facts and evidence. She has much self-confidence and very good speaking skills. In short, Laura is a very good student with much academic promise.

In addition to being a fine student, Laura is blessed with a very fine character. She is intelligent, honest, thoughtful, compassionate and considerate. She is respectful of the rights and feelings of others. She is very sensitive to the plight of others. She is committed to her Christian moral values and tries to live her life based on such values. Laura is a trustworthy and responsible individual; she is also willing to cooperate with the decisions of all for the common good. Laura gets along well with others, and at times she leads in group situations.

Laura would be an asset to any college she attends, both academically and otherwise. Any financial aid offered to Laura would be money well invested.

College Advisor

Recommendation for Kelly

The image of wings over water. The flight is effortless. The reflection clear and moving on the glass lake below. The soft call of the morning breaks the silence of the day. Wings spread, the weightless figure rides the current with knowledge, cutting a clean arc across the clear mountain sky. Precise, efficient, expressive, purposeful. The flight of light has begun. The blue canvas speaks. She is moving/still. She is the light within her.

Kelly is at the threshhold of experience. She is a strong emerging artist with a voice that is firm yet eloquent, directed yet curious, reflective yet probing. Over the past two years in photography Kelly has consistently engaged her work with enthusiasm, thoughtfulness, creativity, and practical determination.

A disciplined craftsperson in the darkroom, Kelly hones a print to perfection while retaining the original vitality of thought. She transposes her fluid skills as a writer to her images on film, and her skill level is apparent. Behind the camera Kelly sees with insight and responds with ready intuition. She works both ends of the process with purposeful expression.

She is experienced with small and medium format film and is well versed in the darkroom and lighting studio. She is equally at home on location or in the studio bringing her sensitivity to content and form to each.

A mature and inquisitive student, Kelly leads her peers by example. Her ideas have weight and texture. Her work ethic is directed and true. In class critiques Kelly is honest, open, direct and supportive.

In other art media Kelly has had less experience, yet I am confident that her creative sensibilities and proven determination will aid her in the acquisition of any new skill. Kelly would certainly excel in your creative community.

Her wings have given her vision. Creativity has come as her guide. Life itself has substance as she breathes in the morning light.

Instructor, Fine Arts Department

HIGH SCHOOL

PRINCIPAL

ASSISTANT PRINCIPAL   ASSISTANT PRINCIPAL

Besides being an extremely fine student,   is just more interesting to be with than most of my students. She likes un-teenage things
like going to art museums or the theater. Granted, she comes from an
interesting family, but many kids do, and they manage to be boring anyway.
          isn't. She's cultured, but at the same time, she's not a nerd.
She's the type who does Outward Bound one summer and a college art class the
next. A neat person.

In order to understand why   is so well prepared for college, you should
know that I worked my students to death in Global Studies English.
read 10 full works of literature in class, including books such as Of Love
and Shadows, A Doll's House, Siddhartha, All Quiet on the Western Front,
and other internationally oriented literature.   also wrote 22 papers:
some historical or research topics, some literary analysis, and a fair amount
of creative writing. I can guarantee that she can write a competent paper.

Besides the aforementioned reading, the students read books outside of class
and wrote on them. I believe you can get a feel for people by what they
choose to read.   read these books last year: The Autobiography of
Malcom X, My Antonia, Black Like Me, Sybil, Beloved, and Fried Green
Tomatoes at the Whistlestop Cafe. Almost all of these books are long and
demanding, an indication of   's love of books, an excellent quality in
a college student, I think.

All in all, I'm very impressed with   as a student and as a person.
She's one student I'd enjoy being friends with ten years from now. She'll
make an excellent college student.

Teacher of English

Dear Sir or Madam:

Jim is a fine, big-tall man with a talent to match and he has energy galore. I have worked with him on several projects over the years here at the art institute and, in fact, Jim was my assistant on a long film project we shot in class. He was great to have around as this gentle-man made everyone feel at ease and feel comfortable in handling the elaborate, syn-sound equipment. He was knowledgeable in all areas of audio/visual exposition and not stingy or constipated in passing that knowledge on to his contemporaries. I have very fond memories of this young man and can heartily endorse him as a welcome attribute to any conglomeration of individuals hell-bent on grinding out motion pictures or learning the process to do so in a painless and productive manner. Jim is tops in my book, and I salute his dedication and good cheer in an ugly business of bloated egos and vicious in-fighting. He shines above them all.

Associate Professor of Film

Recommendation for Bill

Bill always drank the last cup of coffee.

In my classroom at the Twin Rivers School, I kept a coffee maker on a table against the back wall. It gave the room a little humanity, it smelled nice, kids donated beans and brought in their own mugs; also, boarding school coffee is pretty foul. Ordinarily, I'd make a little too much. We'd be left with an inch of blackening, thickening mud at the bottom of the pot. Then, with five minutes to go in class, Bill would rise, pour the motor oil into one of my mugs, sit down and, to my horror, pour it immediately down his poor throat. Why? I asked one day. "When it's cooled off, you can drink it really fast." Then he laughed. Bill's laugh is a unique event. It's about three parts guffaw, two parts rue and all humility. To Bill nothing is funnier than his own peccadilloes. That's what makes him one of the most memorable students I've ever had. That Bill is keenly intelligent, humane, assiduous and perceptive is, I'm certain, well established in his course materials and other references. Bill is not a fast worker. This is not to be confused with a slow mind. His ability to draw connections between events and themes is unparalleled. His political and social sensibilities demonstrate sophistication and sympathy. He shines in class discussions, in which he consistently speaks with both courtesy and conviction—a rare combination.

I never gave a test or exam in which Bill was not the last to finish. And, almost without exception, I never got a result from any other student that was stronger than Bill's. He writes with clarity and great common sense. While reading Mark Twain's *"Letters From The Earth"* in American Studies, we discussed the genre of satire, and each student wrote a satirical piece. Just home from a road trip to the midwest, Bill produced an essay on Minnesota that had me howling with laughter, and which closed with a statement at once so funny and so profound that it vaulted the entire piece into the top half-dozen or so I'd ever received. I still have a copy of it.

Bill's written request for this recommendation, sent to me here in my new California home, was as evocative of his spirit and smarts as anything else. He asked if I was hanging out on Rose Street, and if I had a rash from wearing groovy black turtlenecks. He gave me the latest news from Twin Rivers succinctly and humorously. And when he asked for the reference, he wrote, "lie if you have to."

I don't have to. Bill would be a splendid addition to any community. It is with immense pleasure and great hope that I offer my recommendation for Bill into the collegiate class.

English Teacher

HIGH SCHOOL

PRINCIPAL

ASSISTANT PRINCIPAL   ASSISTANT PRINCIPAL

entered our school system from   Massachusetts, for her
freshman year. I remember her shock in discovering that we did not offer
women's soccer as a varsity sport. The shock turned into determination to
change this, and this new freshman was in the forefront of the movement that
changed our school board policy. As a result of her unusually mature
approach to this issue,   has three years of varsity soccer on her
record, and   had a championship team this year. I was impressed
with   's poise and understanding of the political process throughout
this campaign, and these strengths should serve her well in the future.

If she could have her dream career,   would be a photojournalist. She
does photography projects for the head of our art department and works for a
local photography shop. She spent six weeks at the   School of
Design last summer studying photography. Fortunately,   has a
practical streak, and realizes that such a career is available to very few,
and so she wants a fine arts background that will allow a wider choice of
jobs. She has shown this practicality before when considering her future.
When she thought she wanted to be a nurse,   asked her physician father
to help place her in a career-orientation program on nursing at a nearby
hospital.   learned that she does not want to be a nurse, and is ahead
because of that knowledge.

Besides playing soccer,   has coached a team of five- and six-year olds.
She has helped to organize our very successful Bloodmobile drives the past
three years, and has been front-page editor of our newspaper for the past
two years.

had a difficult junior year, earning her worst grades ever. She has
bounced back nicely this year, with first trimester grades of "C" in Honors
English 12, "C+" in Honors Comparative Government, "C" in Physics, "B-" in
Algebra 3/Trigonometry, "C" in Honors Spanish IV, and "A" in Independent
Study Art (Photography). She has poise and common sense rarely found in one
so young, and a well-thought-out goal for herself.   is a charming
young lady who has won my hearty recommendation.

Guidance Counselor

When I first met Herbert   three years and over fifty pounds ago, he was a smart, shy boy. He moved to   to live with his dad and brother part way into his ninth grade year to leave a bad family situation with his mother in   . Many students at   High School have known each other since elementary school and Herbert was not only a newcomer, but he was being forced into the shadow of his brother, a senior at   and the school nerd. Over the past three years, I have seen Herbert shrink physically, grow academically, and create a social life for himself that causes many to marvel at the fact that he's   's brother.

I first watched Herbert come into his own towards the end of his ninth grade year. Two boys had transferred into my first year Algebra class late in the year because of a conflict with their previous teacher. These two boys had many gaps in both their math knowledge and confidence. Herbert spent a great deal of time working with them to catch them up. For these two boys, Herbert was a lifesaver. He was able to get them back on track in a way that made them feel good about their math ability and fortunate to have met someone like Herbert. I was in awe of how well Herbert was able to connect with these two boys. Rarely have I seen students who require help from a contemporary who have actually gained confidence from that peer. What I didn't realize until later was that this opportunity allowed Herbert to not only share his math abilities and great gift of teaching, but also to have a shot at being social in a new, trying environment. Herbert came to me towards the end of the year concerned about the progress of Stu and Roger. When I assured him that they were both doing well, he got to the root of his question, "Ms.
        will they be able to move on to Geometry with me next year?" At that point, I realized just how vulnerable Herbert was and was amazed at how hard he was working to make   his new home.

Sophomore year,   doubled up in math to create a greater challenge for himself. Through math club which I advise and in which Herbert is an active participant, I kept abreast of his progress. Herbert enjoyed the challenge of two math classes and never missed an opportunity to assure me that he was at the top of both classes.

In his junior year, I had the good fortune to be Herbert's teacher once again, but this time in International Baccalaureate Math Analysis. Academically, it was quite obvious that   belonged in the advanced math track. In this advanced class Herbert was able to banter back and forth with other bright students, and his quick wit and fun side of his personality truly came out.

It was also during this year that I saw Herbert's true genius come to the fore: his computer programming skills. With the introduction of graphing calculators in the classroom, we as teachers often fear that the students will know less math as they become dependent upon their calculator programs. Herbert not only knows his math but has truly mastered the underlying concepts and special cases of every trigonometric rule as is evidenced by the fact that he has actually written the calculator programs that he uses, many of which I have loaded onto my own personal calculator and on which I have come to rely.

One of Herbert's goals, to help others, continues to exist just as it did in his ninth grade Algebra class.   has borrowed the models of the graphing calculator that he does not own from me so that he can rewrite his programs to make them accessible to all students. Entire math club meetings have been devoted to Herbert teaching the math club how to use these programs. Herbert has also come to my current ninth grade Algebra class to help students who are first learning the basics of how to use the graphing calculator. After his first visit, one student came up to tell me how great Herbert's help was and to ask if he would be returning the following day. It is a true testament to Herbert that he is able to help his peers and his teachers in such a way that we all feel grateful to have had him as a teacher in some capacity. Herbert has grown tremendously in the three years that I have known him, and despite his new found acceptance at   High School, he continues to hold on to his basic values which allow him to help and affect the lives of all who he encounters.

I highly recommend Herbert for a scholarship. I am confident that Herbert will shine academically and be a contributing member to the university campus community. Please do not hesitate to contact me if you have any questions or if I can be of further assistance.

Sincerely,

School Letter for

Class leader, sophisticated reader and thinker, varsity athlete, articulate speaker and writer, sensitive student of history and enormously talented individual,   ias taken a demanding college preparatory program including, in his senior year, Humanities, Calculus, Physics, Philosophy (one of our very few college level honors courses), Jazz Ensemble and Photography. He has also led a student/faculty environment team in maintaining our historic landmark building and has been instrumental in planning our annual Martin Luther King Jr. Day celebration, helping secure speakers, films, gospel singers, and organizing interclass discussion groups.

A description of   ,chool may help in assessing   The   . is committed to offering students an integrated course of study in college preparatory core courses as well as coursework and performance in music, theater, dance, and the visual arts. We have a strong international studies program with language classes in Russian, Japanese, and Spanish as well as student exchange programs. Our International House dormitory houses both foreign and domestic students. The school is also concerned with educating students about their environmental and social responsibilities. All seniors, as part of their Humanities requirement, work on behalf of a political candidate or issue; in addition, a comprehensive thesis is required of before they may graduate.

          has taken an active part in all aspects of the school. Some quotes from his teachers will give insight into his abilities:

"...you have been both focused and active in class discussions. You clearly have a good mind for following these arguments and developing your own thoughts in response to what you have read and heard. Your essay on "sophisticated Athenians" (a nice pun) was well crafted and well argued...Keep up the good work!"
(Philosophy)

"   You have devoted yourself to completing this project with excellence. Your precis were carefully done...You skillfully address five of the authors...and you introduce important further perspectives as well. I was particularly impressed by the precision of your analysis when you explored the global connections between rampant, almost patriotic, consumerism within the U.S. and the atrocious denial of human rights that is carried out in the developing world, often in the service of capitalism...Congratulations"
(Humanities)

"   , you have a great brain...some truly intricate and complex thought occurs. Thank you for your willingness to...share it with us."
(Chemistry)

"   is our lead trumpet player; a returnee, he now takes responsibility for the section and has done well in that capacity. His sound is solid and he is reading well...Orion has no idea how good he can be."
(Jazz Ensemble)

"...This is exactly what   did. With all the self-assurance of a graduate student,   set up shop with our feline skulls, made measurements, drew supporting illustrations, developed a mathematical analysis...In short, he carried out a fine comparative anatomy investigation..   's methodology was sound from the start, and he explained it beautifully in a well organized paper."
(Biology)

There is so much that I want to say about   He is truly excited by ideas and loves to discuss them; he is coordinated and graceful on the basketball court and on stage; and he is an intuitive and accomplished musician.   is sometimes too much of a perfectionist, yet he treats his classmates with respect and does not judge them as he does himself. He has worked with and has love for kids and animals, and they treat him like a pied piper.

Most of all,   creates community with his quiet leadership. A recent example clearly demonstrates this. Not long ago,   was one of several students of color from the upper school who participated in a discussion with one middle school student who had repeatedly come into conflict with two of his classmates.   was somewhat subdued during most of the discussion--in which the middle school student voiced sincere but extreme disrespect for homosexuality and homosexuals, and claimed this as a justification for most of his hostile actions. As the discussion came to a close,   leaned forward and simply said to this student: "You have the power to figure out another way to deal with this." In combination with the other students' messages, this comment was stunning. And coming from   , whose stature in the upper school was already significant, it was profound. His power at this school has been rooted in his thoughtful and confident dealings with people.

          has also been a member of   (our multi cultural club). While often too fully engaged with his studies and sports to attend all the regular meetings, he always supported this group's activities by helping out tirelessly at car washes and by attending the events with lots of friends. Last year he agreed to contribute to the   newsletter by interviewing   regionally renowned musician and teacher, about his experience with the early development of be-bop in   .   was initially reluctant to make the commitment because of all that was going on in his life, but once he accepted the assignment he prepared for the interview by reading up on the history of jazz and he conducted the interview for close to an hour and a half. His write-up was engaging, and his own response to talking with   was electric; he was very glad he'd made the effort and had learned a great deal from the meeting and his research beforehand. The feeling was apparently mutual, as   remarked a few days later about how much he'd enjoyed talking with   , and how glad he was that students like   , who care about history, were active in this sort of group.

It is with great enthusiasm that I recommend   , a young man of significant substance, to you.

Very truly yours,

Director of College Counseling

Form Letters

■ Get the college's name right when you send the same letter to vastly different schools.

■ Don't send virtually identical letters for several students to the same college.

■ Tell them something new- describe unique qualities of the student.

We can read this information on the
application. Nothing new, interesting, or
helpful here!

asks for an evaluation of the candidate's academic motivation and promise, as well as any comments you would like make about her character and personality.

(For purposes of confidentiality, all written recommendations in support of the candidate for admission will be used for the admission process only and will be destroyed after the admission decision has been made. The student will not have access to this information. No recommendations will become a part of any enrolling student's permanent file.)

Based on records: This student is active in the following school activities: National Junior Honor Society
Presidential Academic Fitness
NJROTC - Drill Team commander,
Thespians Platoon leader

Community: Craft fairs, Blood donor, Helped with
college night, concession sale, parades, color guard
performances, elementary flag presentations
Church youth group (secretary) summer youth
celebration)
United Way (Day of Caring)
Ninth Grade Orientation)

School District of

March 5

To Whom It May Concern:

This letter of recommendations is written on behalf and at the request of Jane. Jane is a very responsible, respectful individual who is self-motivated and very active in extracurricular activities. Jane was a Rotary Exchange Student and spent her junior year abroad in Ecuador. She speaks fluent Spanish and while there, excelled in her academics. She exhibits leadership qualities and is sensitive to the needs of others. Jane seeks to be in a field that will show her aptitude in serving humanity and being educationally challenged.

Jane was the valedictorian in her junior high school class and the recipient of the American Legion Auxiliary award. She was an Honor Society member and also received various school awards in sports and academic organizations.

I highly recommend Jane to your program without reservation.

Sincerely,

Counselor

NOTE:
All obvious—easily seen on student's application and transcript.

Senior High School

To Whom It May Concern:

I have had the pleasure of working with   for the three years he has attended
         High School.   is a wonderful young man. He is friendly and considerate.
He is an academically able student. He would be a fine addition to the   University
student body. I recommend him to you without hesitation.

Sincerely,

School Counselor

If yes, please list_____

CONFIDENTIAL WRITTEN EVALUATION

_____ asks for an evaluation of the candidate's academic motivation and promise, as well as any comments you would like to make about her character and personality._

or purposes of confidentiality, all written recommendations in support of the candidate for admission will be used for the admission process only and will be destroyed afte the admission decision has been made. The student will not have access to this information. No recommendations will become a part of any enrolling student's permanent file.

HAS DEMONSTRATED THE ENTHUSIASM AND DESIRE TO CONTINUALLY CHALLENGE HER ABILITY AS A WAY OF ATTAINING HER ACADEMIC POTENTIAL. WILLINGNESS TO ACCEPT NEW METHODS OF LEARNING, THE CULTURAL EXCHANGE PROGRAM (SPAIN), CLEARLY SHOWS HER INTEREST IN EXPANDING HER ACADEMIC TALENTS. TENDS TO BE QUIET BUT OPENLY EXPRESSES HER INSIGHTS AND OPINIONS WHEN CALLL ON. IT IS MY SINCERE HOPE THAT ACCEPTS WHICH WOULD BE AN ASSET TO YOUR CAMPUS

School Districts of

January 30

To Whom It May Concern:

Ryan has been a fine student here at Windy High School. He has managed to balance an academic "load" with extracurricular activities and part time work in the family business.

Ryan is a personable young man that is well thought of by both faculty and peers. As a senior, Ryan pursued on his own, an option to take courses at Smart College. This demonstrates the motivation and desire to further himself that Ryan possesses.

I feel very strongly that Ryan will be a successful college student. Please afford him this opportunity.

Sincerely,

Counselor

School Districts of

January 30

To Whom It May Concern:

Susie has been an outstanding student at Sunflower High School. She has managed to be a key member of the school's Oriental Club and honor society. Susie has always worked part time to help support herself and her family, but has still maintained a perfect 4.0 grade point average.

This student has undertaken the challenge of two advanced placement courses this year in calculus and biology. This is normal for Susie. She is a very determined student who never "backs down" from a challenge and works tirelessly at all of her endeavors. Her leadership qualities are well known and she is an officer in Sunflower's AFS program. I believe it is also significant to mention the role that Susie plays at home as a translator for parents.

Susie will be an asset to any institution which affords her admission. Please consider her for this opportunity.

Sincerely,

Counselor

School Districts of

January 30

To Whom It May Concern:

I have known Wendy for a period of three years. She has truly been an extremely "well-rounded, outstandingly talented" academic student here at Blue Sky High School.

Wendy not only is a key member of the school's radio station, the school service committee, and AFS, she is news editor of the school's newspaper. Wendy is also president of the National Honor Society, a member of the Spanish Honor Society, as well as a participant in the Math Club, Quiz Bowl, and Science Olympiad, all while working part time at the local grocery store.

This student is truly a great candidate for admission to your institution. She has a warm personality and a refreshing sense of humor to go along with her dedication to her tasks and perseverance. Her achievement in classes which presently has earned her a perfect 4.0 GPA and her involvement in her school community make her prospects for success tremendous.

Sincerely,

Counselor

This letter is in support of _Steven_ an art student at _School_ Arts. We've been able to work with _Steve_ the last two years & have discovered that _he_ is talented, skilled and enthusiastic about _his_ art work. _He_ accepts challenges, works hard and follows through with _his_ work. _His_ ideas are original and unique.

Steven attitude is excellent. _He_ accepts criticism and goes further in developing _his_ ideas. _He_ will be a definite asset at any college or art school.

Thanks for listening,

Art Instructors
School of

NOTE:
This letter is probably the most blatent example of a form letter. The underlines are part of the letter with the recommender filling in the name of the student and the appropriate gender pronoun.

NOTE:
This letter merely restates information found on the application and transcipt.

and I have known each other for two years in a student-counselor relationship. Academically   has been enrolled in honors and international baccalaureate classes during her four years at our school and has maintained above a 3.0 grade point. Currently her grade point is 3.31 and this week will be reflected on the new transcript to be mailed next week.

played volleyball her freshman year. Outside of school she competed in horse shows, dressage, jumping, and equitation.

The school activities in which   has been involved are: Interact, Future Business Leaders of America, and Big Brothers-Big Sisters. In addition to the above,   works as a waitress at   .

is a young woman with the intellegence and skill to manage many things at one time. Her quiet determination to start a task and see it through has won my admiration.   is a candidate worthy of your consideration.

It is my pleasure to write a letter of recommendation for   , a senior student at   High School. As   's guidance counselor I have gotten to know her quite well this year.

        is ranked 157/457 in her class and has a cumulative GPA of 3.29. She has taken a college core preparatory curriculum and maintained above average grades.   is very interested in the field of law and would like to pursue a career in that area.

        is extremely involved in our soccer program at   High School and has been an asset to the team. She is also involved in the DARE program for younger students. In addition, she volunteers her time at church. She focuses much of her energy working with the less fortunate.   has a reputation for being accountable and committed. She is a very positive and bright young woman.

I think   would make an excellent addition to   University. She is very interested in the Pre-Law and Psychology programs there. I recommend   to your program at   University.

Sincerely,

Counselor

Need We Say More...

- Poorly Written
- Irrelevant
- Unprofessional

SCHOOL DISTRICT

BOARD OF EDUCATION
President

Vice-President

Members

This hurt the student. It was so bad we questioned it's authenticil

Dear Sir:

I cang without hesitationg recommend for your college. He is a fine young man with a lot of potential.

Sincerelyg

, English and history teacher

To whom it may concern:

I am pleased to write in strong support of the application of   to
College.

I have known   since the fall of   , when I joined the faculty of
During the past year and a half,   has had contact with me as a member of the
Chorus, Chamber Singers (a select mixed choral group), and The   (an award-winning
all-male singing group -   was one of its founding members) and as a student in my
Musicianship and Composition class. This semester, these performance groups and classes
amount to fourteen contact periods per week.

In a class that includes several individuals with extraordinary gifts,   stands out as an
extremely talented, creative young man. He is an important member of the bass section in Chorus,
with a voice of true solo quality, well-trained from his days as a member of the
He enthusiastically provides musical leadership to those around him and consistently
brings fine musicianship to his work in ensembles and classes.

        is an artist. He is meticulous, working steadily at his own pace, with very clear ideas
of what he wants to express and how he wants to express it. In addition to his accomplishments in
music,   is an outstanding visual artist and an accomplished actor. He is remarkably
expressive, bringing insight and well-placed emotion to his performances. This semester,
gave up his one free period to take an advanced acting course - not for credit, but simply for the
experience.

        has an excellent sense of responsibility to the communities to which he belongs. He
has served well as Co-Director of Publicity this year in Chorus, and is always willing to give
creatively of his time. In order to publicize this fall's production of Antigone,   co-wrote and
performed a hilarious parody of Spanish Opera. The parody and the show itself were extremely
successful, due largely to   efforts.

In summary, I believe that   <u>meets or exceeds your admission requirements.</u> He
is very talented, focused, outgoing, intelligent, and highly motivated. His artistic accomplishments
and relationships with those around him reflect a maturity beyond his years. In my view, he
would be an excellent addition to your community.

Sincerely,

NOTE:
Otherwise good letter,
but College Admissions
Officer read this underlined
phrase as arrogant,
presumptuous, and rude.

horrible

University of Project Sound
1500 North ~~Jasner~~ Street
~~Tacoma~~ WA. 98416-0003

To: Dean of Admission

It is my sincere pleasure to recommend
        for admission to the University Of Puget Sound.
By every standard,   , is one of the most outstanding
students who ever attended .   High School. Her
achievements are remarkable. I have known   since
ninth grade. I have watched her mature and excel in my
Language Arts Programs. She was a student in Honors English
I and currently, enrolled in my Advanced Placement English
Course now. *redundant*

        I recognized her early mature leadership qualitites and
abilities to balance an academic and athletic career. She
has been a member of the California Scholarship Society for
four years, active player on the tennis team for four years,
on student council for three years and the   President
of the Teachers of Tomorrow Club. She was an
active/founding member of the Teachers of Tomorrow Club's
inception in her freshman year. She's organized fund
raisers, career fairs, theatrical and cultural events for
students. While maintaining an high grade point average.
                frag
        has demonstrated a commitment to the total *left out such word*
school program. Her eloquence, patience, ~~comarderieship~~ and
academic abilities have contributed to her success.

        's ~~supportatiive~~ family members and friendly
mannerism make her a strong candidate to achieve great
~~inroades~~ in life.

        I recommend   without reservation and consider
her to be one of the finest young ladies in   . If I
can be of further assistance to Melanie please let me know.

Sincerely,

        Language Arts Department
Advance Placement English

NOTE:
College Admissions
Officer's comment at
bottom of page.

COUNTY PUBLIC SCHOOLS

February 10

Sirs;

It is at times like this when my lack of command of the English language becomes most obvious and frustrating. Yearly I complete recommendation forms and write letters of recommendation for students and previous students. Usually it boils down to a routine. "This student is an academic achiever." "That student is a leader." Etc. Etc. Etc.

On occasion one student comes along. That student is not the top academic achiever of the class. That student is not president of the student body. That student is "just" an above-average, honest, hard-working, reliable, personable individual. And yet, there is more. There is more to this individual than I am capable of expressing. _____ is such a individual.

I am at a total loss for words to describe _____. She will succeed. It is her nature.

I wish you had tried. You have said next to nothing about her.

THIS IS ALMOST UN-PROFESSIONAL SHE DESERVED TO BE DESCRIBED. AND SHE WASN'T

Department of Art

February 28,

Dear Graduate Admissions Committee,

           was a student in my printmaking class at the   . I remember his prints and him; I was mpressed with not only his drawing skills, but the breadth of his approach.   is very intelligent, well-educated and nnovative. It's a good time for him to go back to school and get his graduate degree. He has been in New York for several years now. He has the motivation and energy to do quite well in the program. I recommend him most highly and think that both the Institute and he will benefit greatly from the interchange.

                 Sincerely,

                 Assistant Professor
                 Department.of Art

credibility?

To Whom it may concern,

I had a student ask me to write him a letter of recommendation. I've had him in three science courses, namely biology, anatomy/physiology, and chemistry. In the city of _____ there are approximately 5000 people. I now know where _____ lives, both his parents, and two of his brothers, all in the last four years.

I live near _____ but I rarely gamble because the odds are in the favor of the casinos. I do like to research a company and perhaps buy a few shares of stock to get a return on my money, which could be considered a type of gambling. _____ could be described as a Blue Chip Stock. He is , in my opinion, gifted. He is also our ASB president. He plays football, basketball, track, and baseball. So what if he has a ridiculous smile and a strange sense of humor, I like him and most people who know him do too.

Seriously, _____ is bright and motivated, particularly in his academic achievement. The University of _____ would be lucky to have him as a future alumni who would do them proud as he already has this high school.

Sincerely,

ps- I have been a science teacher for eight years, I hold a bachelor degree in biology with a minor in chemistry. I have a master's degree in secondary education with an emphasis in biology.

Damning with
Faint Praise

These letters appear supportive
on the surface but...

Antioch • Babson • Bard • Barnard • Bates • Beaver • Beloit • Bennington • Bentley • Boston University • Bowdoin • Brandeis • ...se Western Reserve • Centenary College • Centre • Claremont McKenna • Clark University • Coe • Colby • Colby-Sawyer • Colgate ...ell College • Dartmouth • Denison • University of Denver • DePauw • Dickinson • Drew • Duke • Earlham • Eckerd • Elizabethtown ...Fisk • Fordham • Franklin & Marshall • George Washington • Gettysburg • Goucher • Grinnell • Guilford • Gustavus Adolphus

Hamilton • Hampden-Sydney • Hampshire Hendrix • Hobart & William Smith • Hofstra Juniata • Kalamazoo • Kenyon • Knox • Lafayette Linfield • Macalester • Manhattan • Manhattanville Millsaps • Moravian • Morehouse • Mount Holyoke Occidental • Ohio Wesleyan • Pitzer • Pomona

Hanover • Hartwick • Harvard-Radcliffe • Haverford Hollins • Holy Cross • Hood • Johns Hopkins Lake Forest • Lawrence • Lehigh • Lewis & Clark Marquette • University of Miami • Middlebury • Mills Muhlenberg • New York University • Oberlin University of Puget Sound • Randolph-Macon

Randolph Macon Woman's • University of Redlands • Reed College • Rensselaer Polytechnic • Rhodes • Rice • University of Richmond • Ripon • Rochester Institute of Technology University of Rochester • Rollins • St. Benedict & St. John's • St. Lawrence • St. Olaf • Salem • Santa Clara • Sarah Lawrence • Scripps • Simmons • Skidmore Smith • University of the South • Southern Methodist • Southwestern • Spelman • Stetson • Stonehill • Susquehanna • Swarthmore • Texas Christian & Trinity College Trinity University • Tufts • Tulane • Tulsa • Union • Ursinus • Valparaiso • Vanderbilt • Vassar • Wabash • Wagner • Wake Forest • Washington College Washington & Lee • Wellesley • Wells • Wesleyan • Western Maryland • Wheaton • Whitman • Whittier • Widener • Willamette • Williams • Wooster • Worcester Polytechnic

SCHOOL REPORT

SECONDARY SCHOOL COUNSELOR EVALUATION

The colleges and universities listed above encourage the use of this form. No distinction will be made between it an ___ rm. The accompanying instructions tell you how to complete, copy, and file your application with any one or several of the colleges. Please type or print in black ink.

TO THE APPLICANT:

After filling in the information below, give this form to your college counselor.

Student name: _____
  Last   First   Middle (complete)   Jr. etc.

Address: _____
  Street   City   State   Zip

Social Security No. (optional) _____

Current Year Courses—Please indicate title, level, and term of all courses you are taking this year: sociology,psychology,
Amer. Govt.,arch. drawing,Finite Math,English4,Economics,
keyboarding,R.O.P.(retail sales)

TO THE SECONDARY SCHOOL COLLEGE COUNSELOR:

After filling in the blanks below, use both sides of this form to describe the applicant.

This candidate ranks _228_ in a class of _304_ students and has a cumulative grade point average of _2.62_ on a _4.0_ scale

The rank covers a period from _____ to _____. If a precise rank is not available, please indicate rank to the
  (mo./yr.)   (mo./yr.)

nearest tenth from the top. The rank is weighted _X_ unweighted _____. How many students share this rank _0_

Of this candidate's graduating class, _60_ % plan to attend a four-year college. High school graduation date: _____

In comparison to other college preparatory students *at our school*, the applicant's course selection is:
  ☐ most demanding   ☐ very demanding   ⊗ demanding ⊠   ☐ average   ☐ less than demanding

How long have you known the applicant, and in what context? _4 yrs. As her Counselor_

What are the first words that come to your mind to describe the applicant? _Mature, Intelligent, gregarious_
Empathetic & people-person

Counselor's name (please print or type): _____
                                                              Signature

Position: _Counselor_ _____

School address: _____ Date:_____

Office telephone: (_____)_____ _____ Office FAX: (_____)_____ _____
            Area Code   Number   Area Code   Number

High School CEEB/ACT Code: ___ ___ ___ ___ ___ ___

Please Note: Attach applicant's official transcript, including courses in progress. Include, if available, a school profile and transcript legend. (Please check transcript copies for readability.)

Please feel free to write whatever you think is important about this student, including a description of academic and personal characteristics. I particularly interested in the candidate's intellectual promise, motivation, relative maturity, integrity, independence, originality, initiative, leade. potential, capacity for growth, special talents, and enthusiasm. We welcome information that will help us to differentiate this student from others.

Please See My Enclosed Letter

NOTE:
Attached letter on next page.

RATINGS (optional):

Compared to other students in his or her entire secondary school class, how do you rate this student in terms of:

No basis		Below Average	Average	Good (above average)	Very Good (well above average)	Excellent (top 10%)	One of the top few encountered in my career
	Academic Achievement				X		
	Extracurricular Accomplishments				X		
	Personal Qualities and Character					X	
	Creativity					X	

I recommend this student: ☐ With reservation ☐ Fairly strongly ☐ Strongly ☐ Enthusiastically

CONFIDENTIALITY:

We value your comments highly and ask that you complete this form in the knowledge that it may be retained in the student's file should the applicant matriculate at a member college. In accordance with the Family Educational Rights and Privacy Act of 1974, matriculating students do have access to their permanent files which may include forms such as this one. Colleges do not provide access to admissions records to applicants, those students who are denied admission, or those students who decline an offer of admission. Again, your comments are important to us and we thank you for your cooperation. These colleges are committed to administer all educational policies and activities without discrimination on the basis of race, color, religion, national or ethnic origin, age, handicap, or sex. The admissions process at private undergraduate institutions is exempt from the federal regulation implementing Title IX of the Education Amendments of 1972.

HIGH SCHOOL

December

RE: SS#

Dear Admissions Officer:

_____ is a very charming, mature, sympathetic, gregarious student. She has been an excellent addition to our Peer Counseling Program due to the fact that she is a 'people-person'.

Academically, _____ has not reached her true potential. She has taken a strong college prep program throughout her years with us.

I believe that _____ is now ready to meet the challenges of collegiate life. She has given me indications that she has the ability and desire to be successful.

Please give _____ every consideration.

Sincerely,

Counselor

Office of Registrar
University of

Dear Sir (Madam)

          . has taken French I, II, and a reading course in
French III with me. During this time I have come to know and
appreciate   for her many wonderful qualities.

     I can not(sic) say that   is a strong student. On the
contrary, she is a rather weak student academically. However,
I feel that she definitely deserves her chance at college and
I hope that she will be admitted.

               is a persistent plugger. She always does her work and
trys(sic) to the best of her ability to keep up with her friends.
She is a very likable(sic) girl and has many, many friends. I
feel that   is intensely loyal and as far as I know completely
trustworthy. I think that she can handle college work provided
that it is not too technical and demanding.

     I sincerely hope and pray that you will give her a chance.
She might not make it but she will definitely try.

               Sincerely,

               (French instructor)

               High School

FROM AN INSTRUCTOR TRYING TO BE CANDID AND TRYING NOT TO TORPEDO THE STUDENT'S APPLICATION

EVALUATION *IS "UNDISTINGUISHED"*

Please feel free to write whatever you think is important about this student, including a description of *academic and personal* characteristics. We are particularly interested in the candidate's intellectual promise, motivation, relative maturity, integrity, independence, originality, initiative, leadership potential, capacity for growth, special talents and enthusiasm. We welcome information that will help us to differentiate this student from others.

is a good, if not great scholar, with a good potential for graduating from college. She is capable of handling most work with a minimum of effort, and all of it if she works hard. The important part is that she visualizes herself as a college student and graduating and I can't argue with that premise, although she'll never be as spectacular as most I have recommended. She will do whatever is necessary to stay in college, and fortunately, she has had the academic preparation to handle most everything, including stress and time-management.   is neither exceptionally mature nor exceptionally juvenile. She has quite high integrity. I would classify her as a follower rather than a leader. She has little originality, and seldom takes the initiative. She has few special talents, and only occasionally shows enthusiasm. She is, however, a hard worker, she is fiercely loyal, especially to friends and causes, and if she can find something that "turns her on", she has good potential for growth. I don't mean this to be a negative recommendation, because   should go to college, and she's a very nice girl and quite capable, but she has very few sparkling characteristics to recommend her. Remember, I have worked quite closely with her for these three years, and have held high expectations for her. She has not let me down so much as she has yet to live up to her potential and what she thinks she is or ought to be. Most schools will be glad to have her as a student, and she will be a good representative alumnus--probably working hard on the behalf of the university. She is a very strong supporter of schools. She simply doesn't stand out, and she has been given ample opportunity to do so.

Ratings

Compared to other college students whom you have taught, check how you would rate this student in terms of academic skills and potential:

No basis		Below Average	Average	Good (above average)	Very Good (well above average)	Excellent (top 10%)	One of the top few encountered in my career
	Creative, original thought		X				
	Motivation		X				
	Independence, initiative		X				
	Intellectual ability		X				
	Academic achievement		X				
	Written expression of ideas		X				
	Effective class discussion		X				
	Disciplined work habits			X			
	Potential for growth		X				
	SUMMARY EVALUATION		X				

Signature _____ *ENGLISH TEACHER* Date November 13,

SECONDARY SCHOOL RECOMMENDATION

       is an intelligent, articulate, interesting student who
has been involved in a rigorous college preparatory program at

appears to have an extensive vocabulary and a deep intellectual
potential. He seems to be focused on what he would like to study
in college and is quite certain about his future goals.   has
stated that the areas of physics and philosophy are in his
prospective future and wants very much to expand his already
detailed knowledge in these disciplines.

There is untapped potential in   academic record. Although
conversational interactions are highly motivated and
interesting, his academic performance appears incongruent with
this. He continually chooses challenging coursework, yet, does not
seem to seriously realize his ability.

   has the ability and intensity to succeed, however due to his
previous academic performance, it would be beneficial to obtain his
second quarter grades in order to make an admission decision.
An admission interview would be advantageous for both   and the
Admission Committee.

Sincerely,

Kitchen Sink Letters

It's not that they're too long - though
many are - but there is a sense of
overkill - beyond thorough.

December

Frank, a student at Mountain Song since seventh grade, has had a tremendous impact on the life of the school. A natural leader in the performing arts, Frank has also put together a solid record of achievement in a very demanding course of study. The following excerpts from his teachers' comments last year should provide a clear impression of his abilities and work habits.

"Frank is a delightful student—bright, witty, original, and hard-working. I can always count on him for a creative idea and an unusual turn of phrase. He has fine insights into the works we read, and shares his questions and ideas in class discussion. I have really enjoyed working with Frank (English 11). His second-semester teacher in the came course adds. "Frank has worked well this spring, grasping many textual details and literary themes with ease. His increasing attention to accurate detail and his good questions and comments serve him well. He writes with enthusiasm and force, and has shown a wonderfully perceptive curiosity about literature."

"Frank's remarkable spirit and festive sense of humor make him a pleasure to teach. He is genuinely interested in history, and although tasks take him a great deal of time, he is always diligent in completing them. His term paper on the origins of the blues represented substantial effort and achievement." (U.S. History)

"Frank's a clever and creative physics student. He is insightful and makes observations that show his comprehension and sense of humor. He is able to play with abstractions and to explain concepts in common language. He has worked consistently throughout this course, and his final project was exceptionally well done." (Conceptual Physics)

"I appreciated Frank's enthusiastic, positive class participation. I commend him on his oral proficiency in Spanish and on his creative final video presentation." (Spanish IV)

" I have enjoyed having Frank in my precalculus class this past year. I know Frank put a lot of time and effort into his work and that these efforts did not produce the desired results. He has to learn to speed up the pace of his work. He is a good problem-solver, but he has to learn that a problem doesn't have to be perfect before he can move on the the next one". (Precalculus)

"Frank's efforts in art this semester have been outstanding. He has excellent drawing skills, and every one of his drawings was beautifully rendered and shaded with total confidence. Each drawing has the added bonus of being stamped with Frank is unique viewpoint and style, which is very mature for someone at this level. The resolution of the background for his content drawing was particularly successful. He has a special way with pen and ink, and his drawing had a dreamy, lyrical quality to it. Even his small exam drawing was powerful because of the drama he created with very dark shadows and effective shading. Frank continued to work at his high level of proficiency and commitment this semester. The image he created for his pastel assignment was a powerful political statement that engendered a lot of student response. His colored pencil drawing was a tour de force of beautiful detail and subtleties. His glue transfer print utilized colored pencil in interesting ways with different kinds of strokes and color overlays. It was an arresting image. His independent projects fufilled the assignment well and utilized nicely elements from his selected artist's work. His exam drawing was dynamically composed." (Art Major)

Frank is one of the mainstays of our music and drama programs. The music teacher, who works closely with him in courses and productions, describes as "phenomenal" Frank's talents, commitment, and contributions. Frank a former member of the Mountain Song Choir, is currently part of their Men's Chorale. He is a strong member of our Chorus, Chamber Singers, and Quaker Oats, a men's acappella/barbershop group. He is a frequent soloist and has had strong lead roles in musical theater productions. He also plays and sings in a rock band and performs many of his own compositions. He will certainly have an impact on the musical life of his new school; he's a franchise player. His college list in many cases overlaps with that of his close friend, collaborator, and fellow band member. It's a lucky music director who gets either or both of these exceptionally talented young men.

Frank also a fine versatile actor. He has the dashing looks of the romantic lead (he recently played Haemon in Anouilh's Antigone) but seems to have the most fun in odd-character roles (he also played a nerd turned rock star in The Apple Tree). His theater teacher praises his talents, commitment, positive spirit, and generous, unfailing energy. She says that Frank takes direction remarkably well. He does "a long take", really hears and understands the suggestion, and then does exactly what is expected. Frank is slower than most to master his lines. He is usually working right down to the wire of dress rehearsals. She has a learning disability herself and suggested that a resource person in college might be able to help Frank develop more efficient memorization techniques.

Frank seems hard-wired to work more slowly and methodically than most. Whether he's spread too thin, too much of a perfectionist, unable to prioritize, or learning disabled, there is no doubt that everything from his GPA to his SATs has taken a hit from his need to work to a different clock. There is also no doubt that with world enough and time his results are consistently superior.

In the best of all possible college scenarios for Frank, some of what is now extracurricular might take place within the context of regular course work. He certainly will profit from concentrating on fewer subjects in college, but Frank would also be helped by a reduced course load. I suggested to his music teacher that Frank might do better if he took five years to complete his studies. This teacher, who has great expectations for Frank shook his head in agreement and said, "Six".

Frank is also a solid athlete, a good soccer player. He is built like a brick wall but is also very agile and mobile for someone so thickly muscular. His coach feels that he could play on a competitive Division III team. Again, time constraints may cause Frank to make tough choices and let some things go.

With all of his talents and skills, it is Frank's character, personality, and temperament that we most abmire and love. He is sure to ennoble and enrich any community he joins, and we will surely miss this thoroughly decent and delightful young man.

School Recommendation for Veronica

Veronica is a truly dedicated and enthusiastic learner who has excelled in many of her endeavors, both in and out of the classroom. Her teachers' written evaluations (some of them quoted below) are full of praises for her sophisticated intelligence, her powerful and effective writing, her openness to new ideas, her eagerness to take on new challenges, and her accepting and tolerant demeanor which empowers her to work well with virtually everybody. Self described as "determined, enthusiastic and committed," Veronica has brought these qualities to her many academic, artistic, and community involvements here at school. Her fine character and exceptional personal qualities have made her a standout member of a very strong senior class.

Veronica enjoys the respect and the sincere friendship of her classmates and teachers and of many of the younger students. She is a natural leader, one whose example inspires others, and her empathy and ability to listen have made her a key factor in the growing success of our student support program, which she helped to establish last year and in which she plays a leading role in her senior year. She is one of the student leaders who organizes and conducts the weekly assemblies in which students and faculty meet together to share announcements, offer commentary on various aspects of school life, share performances, and be attentive and amazingly respectful audiences for formal presentations by artists or speakers invited to the meetings. Outside of school, Veronica has been a tutor and a caretaker for three children with very special emotional and developmental needs since she was in 8th grade! This is, for Veronica, not a job done for compensation, but a long-term commitment to help these children and their single-parent mother, and that experience has profoundly influenced her thinking about her future studies and her possible life's work. Realistic enough to know that more education may change some of those goals, Veronica is calm and level-headed and open-minded about that possibility. Perhaps that portrait best captures Veronica's presence here at school: remarkably competent in so many areas, yet calm and even tempered and simply getting her many jobs done with true joy and good humor. She is an outstanding young woman who I enthusiastically recommend to the school of her choice.

------ School incorporates a college preparatory program, extensive study abroad opportunities, classes in both the performing (music, drama, dance) and visual arts, and a variety of community service offerings. In here years here at ------ School, Veronica has pursued a rich and varied curriculum, including: four years each of English, social studies and lab sciences; four years of math, culminating in Statistics; four years of Spanish, and a variety of arts classes including dance, music, drama, and the visual arts. In addition, Veronica is doing an outstanding job as a senior natural helper; she has been also been a leader in community service projects.

Veronica's own teachers, in their written evaluations of her work, speak of her remarkable growth, academic achievement, and peer leadership in their classes: "Your work, participation, and self motivation to learn are nothing short of excellent. Your class work and homework are thorough, your attitude is positive, you have a wry sense of humor which serves you well. Your essays are creative and solid. They consistently express profound ideas in a style which is highly mature and readable. With regard to discussions, your are an eager and active participant, both strong in your own opinions and diplomatic in listening to others." (English 10) "Veronica, congratulations are In order for your strong finish to the year in this class. You have done a great job of trying hard, getting help and working though frustrations when applications did not come easily for you. Your work was consistently very neat and well organized, making it easy to follow your problem-solving strategies. This taking ownership of your learning set a great example for the others. Thank you!" (Geometry) "Veronica's work with genetics this semester was excellent. She clearly understood what was going on. Her final paper on fertility-enhancement drugs was terrific. The rough draft needed very little work, and the final paper was solid - readable, intelligent, and well referenced. I'm glad to be able to reflect in the grade below [A], Veronica's real capabilities in Biology." (Biology) "Veronica, un ano fantastico! You enthusiasm and consistency in this class throughout the year were highly laudable. You improved immensely in your confidence and ability to write and speak Spanish. Your investigation was fantastic!" (Spanish II) "Most of all, in this class, I wanted to see you make connections between the culture and the dance that grew out of it. You did this beautifully in your extra-credit report on "Forever Tango"...[which] was characteristic of your involvement in the class all year. Your written work has been superb, your kindness and enthusiasm contagious, and your leadership helpful. Thanks for a great year!" (Folk Dance) "Veronica gave wonderfully commanding performances as the harried but domineering Madame Jordaine in our outdoor production of *The Would-Be Gentleman*...Her sense of timing and her ability to include the audience were masterful and she made clear progress from earlier, more simple and direct work as Rebecca Nurse in *The Crucible*." (Drama) "Clearly you do outstanding work in all aspects of this course. Your essays are excellent in all terms of concept, style, mechanics, and substantiation. Without question, your best essay this semester has been the one about *The Great Gatsby*. It is profound and stunning. On another note, I very much appreciate your leadership in class discussions. It is an honor to work with you." (English 11) "Veronica! Nice job in chemistry this term. Despite your expressed hesitation about all this, you've made the most of your time and your study in here, and, hopefully, you recognize how much you've accomplished. You obviously have had no difficulty with the daily concepts in here, you're coming along nicely with your lab skills, and your communications of your work in the lab is also nicely done. Keep up the great work." (Chemistry) "Veronica, another great term! You are an exceptional student to have such command of the language in a few years of study. Your paper on the situation in Mexico City was clearly written in a sophisticated style. Great point that the girls don't have the dignity which we take for granted!" (Spanish V) "Wow! Such exquisite images of hands and beautifully presented. You really went the extra mile this term and it shows. All of your images are beautifully composed and the printing is superior. The hands as triptychs on mat board are wonderful! You really put a lot of thought into the presentation." (Photography) "Thanks again for your unfailing support and enthusiasm for our program. Your style at weekly assemblies has been such a positive way for the community to know that student supporters are cool, smart, and fun. Your opinions have been a source for many of the changes we will be implementing next year." (Leadership) "Veronica is unique in the universe, an actress who is willing to go way out there, which gives her and us so much to build upon. She serves as a model of courage and daring for the group." (Advanced Drama) "Veronica is simply and clearly one of the best writers in this class. Each of her shorter reflections is carefully written, clear in its expression, and full of insight and understanding. I have truly enjoyed reading each of those pieces, and Veronica's voice comes across distinctly in each one. Her personal statement was terse and direct and covered a surprising range of topics. Veronica's self confidence in this kind of writing is notable. She simply thinks well and writes well about important questions and issues. And her comments in class discussion have helped to keep us on track or to shed light from a new perspective." (English 12)

As the above quotes amply reveal, Veronica is exceptionally well qualified to embark upon her post-secondary studies with the same enthusiasm and passion and success she has demonstrated and experienced here. I heartily recommend her to the school of her choice with full confidence that she will be a welcome addition to the school community she joins next fall.

Sincerely

Teacher Recommendation for

        is the hardest working student I have ever met.   has only been in the US for a year and a half. She learned English faster than any other student I have encountered. By the end of my course, she was writing some of the most accomplished papers in the class. Within a year, she was outperforming most of the native speakers.   learned English through hard work. Her Chinese-English dictionary was constantly at her side. She looked up every word she encountered that she did not know. When she first took tests, she wrote out the answers in Chinese and then translated them into English. She did this in the same time it took American students to complete the test.   was meticulous about completing every assignment. It often took her twice as long to complete the work as American students. For instance, she had at least 25 pages of reading a night.   had to look up many words in order to complete the reading. Even so, she would frequently makes notes to herself in the margins to ask me the next day when she returned to class.

        also overcame her initial shyness about speaking English. At first, when she spoke in class, she was so quiet that I had to repeat her statements to the class. Students could not understand what she was saying and told her so. However,   persisted in speaking in class and her elocution and volume improved. By the end of the class, other students acknowledged her for making some of the most valuable contributions to class discussion.   did in fact make some of the profound statements of the year. When our class was debating whether classes should be tracked by ability,   replied that a class is like birds singing in the forest. If only the most accomplished birds in the forest sang, the song would not be as beautiful. I am not sure if it is because   speaks English like she speaks Chinese, or whether she has an innate sense of poetry, but her writing and speech had a lyrical quality. Some of her phrases and stories were exquisitely beautiful.

        She has a deep understanding about life.   is much wiser than her years. Her experiences of living in different countries has made her strong. The last years   spent in China, she lived alone. Her parents had both gone overseas to take jobs that would enable them to leave China. As a young teenager,   had to fend for herself. Her grandfather would visit her on Sundays and take her shopping for food for the week. However, when a crisis arose,   had to rely on her own resources to handle it. She overcame the loneliness of coming home to an empty house. She did her homework even though there was no one around to tell her to do it.   learned the true meaning of self-motivation. She understood that the point of learning was to enlarge her understanding so that she can live well.

        has learned to be at peace with herself. Because she spent so much time alone, relying on her inner resources, she is extremely self-aware. Overcoming the tribulations of leaving her homeland and moving to two different continents to start a new life, has given her a quiet confidence and indomitable determination.   arrived in the US in June. In September, she started classes at   To teach herself English, she rented movies.   watched over 200 movies in her first year in the US. I have never met a student more determined to learn English. She tirelessly rewrote papers until they were A quality work. She asked me to edit her daily journal entries. She constantly corrected her mistakes until she had internalized perplexing points of English grammar. The fact that within a year she was outperforming many native speakers indicates the depth of her intellectual potential.   took AP classes her first year in this country. For example, she took AP chemistry because the formulas were easy for her to grasp.   excels in math and she used this ability to help her learn English through her science classes. This year,   took AP language arts. Most students who have been in the US for a year are still in ESL classes.

        . also become involved with extracurricular activities. For example, she will become a staff leader in the outdoor program at   this year. She has completed basic and advanced wilderness survival training programs. She is a member of Future Leaders of America. She was a national judge for one competition last year. She also won a contest for obtaining the most sponsors for a school clean-up.   is also in the Honor Society at also supports her community by volunteering. She tutors at the   elementary school two hours a week. She is currently developing a program to involve other Future Leaders for America students in tutoring at elementary schools.   also volunteers at the   Medical treatment center every Friday. She is planning a trip to Mexico to help build houses for homeless people with her youth group.   volunteers for the   Christian Association for three hours a week and teaches Sunday school.   is a profoundly spiritual young woman. She believes that helping others is the path to ultimate happiness. She is extremely kind and considerate of others. She can see positive qualities in everyone she meets.   appreciates students who have extremely different values than her own. For example,   is extremely gentle and polite. However, she relates well to my students who are aggressive, curse loudly and act disrespectfully. She can see past their behavior to what she believes is their essential goodness. As a result,   brings out the best in them. I was always astounded by how politely some of my most difficult students were when they spoke with   wants to be a doctor to help others. She wants to uplift their spirit as well as heal their bodies. She had an extremely postive impact on her classmates and I have no doubt that she will bring peace as well as health to her patients.

        is talented in many different areas. She is an accomplished pianist and artist. She is quite competent with computers and studies AP Physics independently.   has extraordinary determination, remarkable intelligence and compassion for others. She will use her finely trained mind and her iron will to benefit others. It is has been a great pleasure for me to have her as a student. She will be a tremendous asset to your program.

        Language Arts Teacher
        High School

NOTE:
Gets bogged down trying to include everything, thereby detracting from an otherwise excellent and insightful academic recommendation.

Sabotage or Brave Teacher?

■   Are these letters too brutally honest?

■   If you can't say something positive, perhaps
you should decline to write on behalf of the student.

We got a laugh out of this one! But, we also appreciate the honesty this teacher expressed.

_____ has great potential and academic ability but does not put forth the needed effort. She failed second semester of my alg II course mostly due to missed days. She has an extreme number of absences which seem without excuse. She says she suffers from migrains, but students say she just likes the sun and soaps during spring time. She seems to lack motivation even when she is in my class. Sometimes she chooses to sleep. She is now repeating Alg II.

Yikes!
This is one of my favorites!

UNIVERSITY

ACADEMIC REFERENCE

STUDENT:

Fill in the information below and give this form and a stamped envelope, addressed to Clark University Admissions Office, to a teacher or professor who has taught you an academic subject.

Student name: _____ ☒ Freshman ☐ Transfer
First   Middle (complete)

Address: _____
Street   City   State   Zip Code

TEACHER:

The Admissions Committee finds candid evaluations helpful in choosing from among highly qualified candidates. We are primarily interested in whatever you think is important about the applicant's academic and personal qualifications for college. Please submit your references promptly. A photocopy of this reference form, or another reference you may have prepared on behalf of this student is acceptable. You are encouraged to keep the original of this form in your private files for use should the student need additional recommendations. We are grateful for your assistance.

CONFIDENTIALITY:

We value your comments highly and ask that you complete this form in the knowledge that it may be retained in the student's file should the applicant matriculate at the University. In accordance with the Family Educational Rights and Privacy Act of 1974, matriculating students do have access to their permanent files which may include forms such as this one. The University does not provide access to admissions records to applicants, those students who are rejected, or those students who decline an offer of admission. Again, your comments are important to us and we thank you for your cooperation.

Teacher/Professor's Name (please print or type) _____ Position _Counselor_

Secondary School/College _____ _High_

School/College Address _____
Street   City   State   Zip Code

BACKGROUND INFORMATION

How long have you known this student and in what context? _3½ years_

What are the first words that come to your mind to describe this student? _gentle, attractive_
sweet, kind, warm, winning ☺!

List the courses you have taught this student, noting for each the student's year in school and the level of course difficulty.

rarely achieves passing
grades in any of her courses.
Because we like her, she is
frequently passed on to another
"desperation"

(See reverse side) TE

EVALUATION

Please feel free to write whatever you think is important about this student, including a description of *academic and personal* characteristics. We are particularly interested in the candidate's intellectual promise, motivation, relative maturity, integrity, independence, originality, initiative, leadership potential, capacity for growth, special talents and enthusiasm. We welcome information that will help us to differentiate this student from others.

has a lot of leadership potential--unfortunately, she leads people in the wrong direction. In the past 3 months, she has had her licgense revoked by the Dept. of Motor Vehicles for speeding violations, and was suspended from the athletic teams for behavior problems. She lost any chance of participating in student gov't. as well. She is careless, reckless, and very unconcerned about the consequences of her actions. There is nothing to comment on in terms of personal maturity and integrity. I do not know of any teacher in this school who has not had a problem with Several teachers have referred   for various things, but she does nothing to straighten herself out. 'Nothing is her fault--everyone is out to get her.' I have never come across a student like her; it has been my experience that students want to improve themselves and grow.   likes being the way she is. Our counseling departemnt has tried everything, including a strong suggestion that she get outside counseling. (This was in Oct/Nov after   assaulted another student). laughs and says she doesn't need help.

LETTERS LIKE THIS ARE RARE! THIS ONE FROM A BRAVE TEACHER MADE A DIFFERENCE

Ratings

Compared to other college students whom you have taught, check how you would rate this student in terms of academic skills and potential:

No basis		Below Average	Average	Good (above average)	Very Good (well above average)	Excellent (top 10%)	One of the top few encountered in my career
	Creative, original thought				✓		
	Motivation			✓			
	Independence, initiative			✓			
	Intellectual ability			✓			
	Academic achievement			✓			
	Written expression of ideas		✓	✓			
	Effective class discussion		✓				
	Disciplined work habits		✓				
	Potential for growth	✓					
	SUMMARY EVALUATION		— —				

Signature _____ FRENCH TEACHER Date 12/1?/0?

EVALUATION

Please feel free to write whatever you think is important about the applicant, including a description of academic and personal characteristics. We are particularly interested in the candidate's intellectual purpose, motivation, relative maturity, integrity, independence, originality, initiative, leadership potential, capacity for growth, special talents and enthusiasm. We welcome information that will help us to differentiate this student from others.

is the most unrealistic student I've ever encountered. She appears to believe she can "wish" herself into the university. The only true effort I've ever seen her exert is the effort she is putting forth in applying to almost 100 universities. I'm exhausted writing her "recommendations". She has little or No academic motivation and only a minimal appreciation of the academic environment. To this day she cuts classes, is frequently late when she does attend, talks incessantly in class, fights with many of her teachers) and I'm worried about even getting her graduated.

RATINGS

How would you rate this student in terms of academic skills and potential:

No basis		Below Average	Average	Good (above average)	Very Good (well above average)	Excellent (top 10%)	One of the top few encountered in my career
	Creative, original thought	✓					
	Motivation	✓					
	Independence, initiative	✓					
	Intellectual ability	✓					
	Academic achievement	✓					
	Written expression of ideas	✓					
	Effective class discussion	✓					
	Disciplined work habits	✓					
	Potential for growth	✓					
	SUMMARY EVALUATION	✓					

Signature _____ Date _____

January 11

Counselor's Recommendation For Susan

Susan is an ebullient, humorous, bright young lady who has done <u>reasonably well</u> in her four years at White Pine. She has taken an average curriculm compared to her classmates and her performance has been <u>good but not great</u>. Susan has made a lasting impression on her teachers and coaches with her sometimes <u>off the wall antics</u>. She can be very enjoyable and fun to work with but she can also <u>get carried away</u> with her goofy behavior and end up being a distraction.

Susan is very creative and she has a great sense of humor. Therefore, it shouldn't come as a surprise that theater has been one of her favorite activities at White Pine. Susan has performed in several school productions, most recently " Tree" in which she carried one of the lead roles. I had the pleasure of watching this play and I must confess that it was probably the best production that I have ever seen at White Pine School. According to her drama teacher, Susan shows lots of initiative in creating a character on stage. She has a very innovative mind and figures out how to develop a character in some very unusual and creative ways. In her work in the theater, Susan's punctuality and attendance for rehearsals has been virtually perfect over the past for years. Recently, she accepted a very small part in "Pin" after another student who wanted a larger role had dropped out. Susan has been the best person in the cast in terms of attending rehearsals and she continually volunteers to fill in for others who are absent.

In her class, Susan has produced some good work but she is <u>inconsistent</u>. Her <u>effort seems to flucuate</u> depending upon her mood. For example, she is more than capable of producing quality work in English, but sometimes her ebullience or occasional boredom can get the better of her. Susan has not yet shown the kind of discipline required to take a draft of a paper and rewrite it a few times in an attempt to create a more perfect final copy. She is often content with a shallow rewrite of her first draft which will often contain some good ideas but there has been <u>very little attention to detail</u>.

Across the board, Susan's teachers make the same remarks about her work. She's bright enough to do a fairly good job, but she often gets caught up in playing the role of the class clown and is completely unfocused on the material at hand. I had the experience of teaching Susan when she was a ninth grader in World History. Without any prompting, Susan would suddenly stand up and burst into a rendition of "The Star Spangled Banner" while the class was in the middle of reviewing a reading assignment on the Middle Ages. All kinds of characters appeared in class. Daffy Duck, Adolf Hitler, and Jim Morrison, among others, possessed Susan's body at some point during the year. Susan can get <u>bored very quickly</u> with the same old classroom routine. She <u>needs to be entertained</u> and if the teacher or other students don't provide this entertainment then she begins creating another character to make things more interesting. It's funny, but she <u>can certainly go overboard</u>.

<u>I think that Susan would be capable</u> of handling the workload at White Water College. She has shown <u>flashes of quality work</u> and her standardized test scores would seem to indicate that she is perfectly bright. However, she has not put in the consistent day to day effort that your admissions committee would probably like to see. She's <u>not a "plugger"</u> or someone who will continually seek extra help

from her teachers. She loves to visit her teachers during the day, but these are usually just social visits. I suspect that Susan would tone things down in the classroom in a college setting. All in all, Susan is well liked by her peers and her teachers. We sometimes get a little frustrated with her but we are usually laughing about it later on. Despite the occasional frustrating experience in dealing with her, her role as the class clown, and her inconsistent effort, I recommend that you offer Susan a spot in next year's entering class. Yes, she's on the goofy side, but Susan <u>may be worth taking</u>.

Respectfully submitted,

College Counselor

Faculty

Strategies for
Students

Strategies for Students...
Requesting Recommendations

Most college applications require students to submit letters of recommendation. In some instances these letters are of little value in admissions decisions, while at other times they may be a deciding factor. A student may think, "I've read the profile of accepted students at the schools of my choice, and I easily fit in, so what difference will letters of recommendation make? Will anyone even read them?" If it were as simple as taking the right courses, obtaining good grades, and earning solid, high scores on the SAT or ACT, the whole process would be a lot clearer. Colleges, however, receive many more applications from qualified students than the number of available spaces. Every additional piece of information that can differentiate one student from another can be very important.

Colleges are interested in knowing the individuals behind the grades. Is this student self-motivated? Does she go one step beyond the assignment or is an 'A' her only goal? What is she like as a student? Equally significant, what is she like as a person? An applicant, therefore, needs to think carefully about which teachers can address these issues most effectively. This section is designed to help students maximize their chances of getting the kinds of recommendations that will be most useful to college admission offices and advantageous to students.

Ask Teachers Who Know You Well...

You may have gotten an 'A' in your history class, but can your teacher say anything more than Suzy got A's on all her tests, handed in her homework on time, and was never late to class? Such observations are not terribly exciting or revealing. Try to think of classes that really excited you. Did they lead to conversations with your teachers that extended to subjects outside of the classroom? Was your teacher also an advisor to a club or committee you were on? Were you an active contributor in class discussions? Had you ever shared your goals or aspirations with your teacher? Did you have the same teacher for more than one course?

It is the teacher who knows you well who will be able to make you come alive to a college admissions committee. It is that teacher who will be able to describe you as a student who will be an asset to the academic and social community of the campus. It is that teacher who will be able to distinguish you from others whose recommendations portray them as good, dutiful students, but do not offer insights into their thinking or character.

Ask an Eleventh or Twelfth Grade Teacher...

You've changed. You've matured. You're not the same person you were in ninth or tenth grade. Even your favorite ninth grade teacher would see you as a student of greater depth and understanding than he did three years ago.

Consider the case of the most popular teacher at "Uniform High School". Each year 150 new students enroll in his classes because of his accessibility to students and his gift for teaching. While you may have been his top student three years ago, the specifics of your classroom contributions may have dimmed, and he is more focused on his current students.

Eleventh and twelfth grade coursework is often more challenging and a better indicator of a student's readiness for a rigorous college program. It is, therefore, more desirable to have eleventh and twelfth grade teachers write letters of recommendation for you whenever possible. They know your most recent work, remember the discussions you've added to the class, and are frequently able to write the most insightful letters of recommendation.

Why this Particular Teacher...

Presumably you have good reasons beyond the grade you received for choosing a particular teacher to write your recommendation. Did a teacher inspire you to learn about a subject in more depth? Did she lead stimulating discussions that you and your friends continued outside of class? Do you have more confidence because of how she demonstrated that she respected you? Was she one of the best teachers you ever had? Once you have considered some of your reasons, ask yourself one more question: Have you ever let your teacher know how much she influenced you?

When you ask a teacher for a recommendation, let her know why you asked her. She probably doesn't know how much you enjoyed her class. Teachers get too few compliments and not enough positive feedback for their efforts. Such a conversation with a teacher may lead to a better understanding of you when she sits down to write your recommendation.

Ask an English Teacher...

Whether you are studying architecture, math, psychology, or physical therapy, to be able to succeed in college you must know how to communicate effectively. Colleges are interested in how you think, how you organize your thoughts, and how you communicate both orally and in writing. Most often, the people who are in the best position to evaluate you in this area are English teachers. Your verbal SAT score may be low, but a strong letter from a Language Arts teacher who can speak to how well you write may reassure the college admissions committee of your skills. In the event you have no English teacher to recommend you- they do, after all, retire, move, change careers, or limit the number of students for whom they can prepare recommendations - a social studies/history teacher would be a good alternative.

Consider Asking...

Were you the star of your school play? Has your premier soccer coach encouraged you to play in college? Did your art teacher submit your work to a regional contest? Did you have a summer internship at a local lab? Have you been working for the same employer throughout high school? Do you devote a significant portion of your time to a volunteer activity?

While teachers of academic subjects are most important to a college admissions officer, coaches, employers, extracurricular advisors, or visual arts teachers can add valuable information to your application package. Such letters of recommendation are in addition to, not instead of, academic letters unless you are planning to concentrate in a given art, such as dance. These individuals interact with you under different circumstances and can offer a professional's perspective about your special talents. They may be more familiar with your aspirations and passions than your academic teachers. They can provide a more well-rounded picture of the unique abilities and qualities you will bring to the college community.

Ask in a Timely Fashion...

Ann rushed up to Mrs. Smith in the hallway. "I need a letter of recommendation right away. I've decided to apply early decision to Greater Metropolis College, and everything is due by Friday."

Diana also wanted a letter from Mrs. Smith but, unlike Ann, knew the request was more than a mere formality. Mrs. Smith had had both of them, each an outstanding student, in her Honors English ll class and found them equally talented. Diana, though, approached Mrs. Smith and asked whether she would be willing to, and had the time to, write on her behalf. She gave Mrs. Smith adequate notice of her earliest due date and let Mrs. Smith know of her willingness and desire to discuss her college plans. From the start, Diana was sensitive to, and appreciative of, her teacher's needs and priorities.

High school students often lose sight of the fact that teachers have lives beyond the classroom and, while most are more than happy to provide letters of recommendation for students, it is important that you, as students, express your appreciation for the extra time they are expending on your behalf. These letters frequently take up to three hours or more to write, because teachers want to present each student in as positive a light as possible. They pen these letters in addition to, not instead of, preparing for classes, teaching, meeting with students, grading assignments and tests, writing evaluations, conferencing with parents, advising school activities, attending faculty meetings, and taking professional development courses.

Say thank you... and mean it.

Provide Teachers with Information...

Before you approach a teacher for a letter of recommendation, think about what you would hope to have her say about you. Then write a short résumé including your goals and aspirations in a clear, concise, easy to read fashion. Teachers appreciate such help. Teachers, particularly those who have honors or AP classes, are asked to write numerous letters of recommendation. Not only do you make it simpler for a teacher when you provide written information about yourself, but you may also be able to impact the tone and scope of the letter.

Imagine a teacher settling down at her desk to write recommendations for 75 students. The chore is certainly daunting. She is desperately trying to remember each student's interests and accomplishments. Did Michael present that outstanding research paper on Thomas Jefferson or did he write about Jefferson Davis? Was it Ilyse who performed in *Romeo and Juliet* or was she in *Guys and Dolls?* Does Scott play the sousaphone or the trombone? Did Deborah say that she's interested in biology or chemistry? Jodi has been hanging around school after classes have ended, but what does she do? Think how that teacher would feel if, instead of just 75 names and 350 recommendation forms, she also had 75 one page summaries for each student. Consider that teacher's mind-set when she gets to your name, and you are the only one who has provided her with some reminders of your activities and goals.

While a teacher's recommendations are necessary for most college applications, it is rarely in her contract to provide them. She may, in fact, determine that she has time to do them for only a limited number of applicants. They are time consuming to write and are often done on weekends or vacations. Anything you can do to simplify the task will likely be beneficial to you.

It's the little things that count, and one way you can expedite the college recommendation process is to provide each teacher who is writing for you with business sized envelopes, stamped and addressed to the colleges to which they are to be sent. Once the letter is written, it will enable the teacher to quickly copy, sign and insert each recommendation letter and form into the appropriate envelope. It will help to organize and simplify the process. The writer, therefore, does not have to search for addresses, nor does she need to spend her own money on stationary or stamps. What caring teacher will delay sending your letters when you've already shown such consideration and spent your hard earned coins on making her job easier?

The Thicker the File, the Thicker the Student...

NOTE:
Do not send extra letters unless they say something new.

"Greg is honest, loyal and trustworthy. He plays soccer, volunteers at the Boys and Girls Club, and has been secretary of the junior class."

"In addition to playing soccer, Greg is a volunteer at the local Boys and Girls Club and has been active in student government. He is sincere and has high integrity."

"Greg is an active participant in the school. He is on the soccer team and is an ASB officer. He also does community service. He is always well mannered and neatly groomed."

College admissions officers are busy people. They must peruse many applications during the reading period. If they have requested two letters of recommendation, they do not want ten, especially when eight of them add nothing new to the your profile. This volume is considered overkill and may actually turn off the college reader. Only when an additional recommendation will add new insights into your abilities, talents, or character, should unsolicited letters be sent. Clearly, however, an employer for whom you've successfully completed a special project, an internship supervisor, an arts director, or a coach may offer a unique perspective of you.

As a general rule, remember the old adage, "the thicker the file, the thicker the student".

Survey

About the Survey

A survey was distributed to colleges and universities to determine the relative weight given to various categories of recommenders. In addition, the importance of students' waiving confidentiality and the value placed on private vs. public school counselor recommendations were explored. Surveys were sent out, and forty-seven of them were returned.

The results of the survey are meaningful for high school and independent counselors in their roles as college placement advisors. Students are also given new insights as to whom to approach for recommendations to colleges.

As expected, when asking teachers of academic subjects to write on behalf of students, 11th and 12th grade teachers are preferred (87.2%) over 9th and 10th grade teachers (0.00%). 12.8% of the respondents viewed each group equally. In addition, there is very little difference (85.1%) in importance as to whether or not one waives confidentiality, and 87.2% of the colleges surveyed weighted recommendations from private and public schools without preference.

While teacher recommendations (24.4%) are more highly regarded than those of counselors (11.1%), on the whole there is little preference for one over the other (64.7%). However, if a school's policy dictates that counselors do not provide recommendations, it can impact a student's application (36.2%). In such instances, it is suggested that the student send an additional letter from a teacher.

Academic teacher and counselor evaluations are definitely the most highly valued ones in the college application process. It is also interesting to note the degree of importance placed on recommendations from other sources. The survey indicated that extracurricular advisors, special talent teachers, and employers may be valuable resources for college admission committees, while recommendations from parents, peers, and family friends are rarely beneficial. Of course, an exception arises when they are requested or a family friend knows the student well and has a strong association with the school. Input from coaches is highly useful when a student hopes to play a sport on the intercollegiate level.

There was uniform agreement that the most beneficial recommendations are those that provide greater insight into a student's abilities, character, and potential. They are most helpful when they add information about a student that cannot be found elsewhere on the application.

Dear Colleague:

During this busy time of year we are more aware than ever of the value of counselor and teacher recommendations. However, there are few guidelines or examples to follow, which makes the task more difficult, more time consuming, and perhaps less reflective than desirable. If a resource existed for writers to consult, not only would recommenders benefit, but so would students and college admissions professionals. We are, therefore, seeking examples of such letters that you have considered valuable, unhelpful, or simply hilarious, to compile into a book. Of course, letters will be sanitized with names of students, high schools, and authors of letters held confidential.

We would appreciate receiving examples of such correspondence with the enclosed checklist and any comments you may care to share. Please feel free to write directly on each recommendation letter. Through this vehicle, we hope to improve the usefulness of the recommendation portion of college applications.

Thank you for providing this data.

Sincerely yours,

Linda Jacobs
Pauline B. Reiter

Name of Institution_____

Contact Person_____

Address_____

Phone_____Fax_____

In addition to submitting samples of recommendation letters, please fill out the following questionnaire.

Please check the item in each row to which you give more weight in the application process or indicate if there is no difference:

1) Confidentiality waived_____not waived_____no difference_____

2) Counselor Rec from public school _____ private school_____ no difference_____

3)Teacher Rec _____ Counselor Rec _____ no difference_____

4) 11th & 12th grade Teacher Recs _____ 9th & 10th grade Teacher Recs _____ no difference_____

Please rate the importance of recommendations from the following sources using a scale of 1 to 5, 1 being not important and 5 being very important:

Coaches_____   Clergy_____   Peers_____

Extracurricular Advisors_____   Parents_____   Well Known Alumni_____

Special talent teachers_____   Employers_____   Community Service Supervisors_____

Long term friends/acquaintances of the family_____

Other (please specify)_____

If a school does not have a college counselor or school policy dictates that counselors do not write recommendations, how does that impact the student's application?

greatly_____   somewhat_____   not at all_____

Any Other Comments:
(Please attach additional sheets if necessary.)

_____

_____

_____

_____

_____

_____

OTHER PUBLICATIONS :

101 Tips for College Bound Students

For additional copies
of College Recommendations

To order one or more copies, please fill out the form below and return it with your check or money order to UNIVERSITY PATHWAYS 5508 35th Avenue N.E., Suite 104, Seattle, WA 98105. Contact UNIVERSITY PATHWAYS for discounts on multiple copies.

Name _____

Address _____

City _____

State and Zip _____

Phone _____

Email _____

Please send me_____copies at $19.95 each

                     AMOUNT _____

                     8.8% SALES TAX
                     FOR WA DELIVERY _____
                     ($1.76 per book)

Add $3.00 for postage and handling   **$3.00**

                     TOTAL ENCLOSED _____

Payment: check or money order, payable to University Pathways